Marco Perino

...what if the BLACK Sheep is me?

Cover image created by Rossella Pitarresi
Graphic design by Andrea "Melaz" Meloni
Translation from original version by Michael Magill

EVERY STORY IS TRUE !!!

IT'S NOT THE FRUIT OF THE AUTHOR'S IMMAGINATION

Marco Perino

March 20, 2017

To all the black sheep ...

I was born a sheep!

I bleat and shit little balls.

I'm like all of you. Not better, not worse. A sheep !

I don't understand why. I was in the flock as usual. I was looking for clumps of grass as usual.

Then something happened.

I felt they're eyes on me.

They looked at me.
They judged me.
They kept their distance from me.

Their black balls were getting farther and farther away from me.

I had stopped and at a certain point I found myself alone.

Why did the flock turn away from me?

ACT ONE

They walked away

"I am the good shepherd; I know my sheep and my sheep know me"

John 10:14

I love to drive when the sun is rising

without worries or dominant thoughts

like pressing play on a CD without a cover

or song title ...

... and then

Shuffle

- Track 9 -

"Come on, let's go ... What's wrong with you? ... Come on, come on ... Wake up ... Let's move!"

It was early morning, I was in bed and he was in front of me all perky; energy bursting from every pore with a face that laughed at me while he spoke. I hated him!

All this was not expected! He wasn't supposed to be here and I should have closed the door last night, I should have also closed the door the night before that; or was it night? It doesn't matter, he shouldn't have come in, even if he tried he couldn't have entered. And then no! Not today! This time I don't want your improvising! This time I wanted a some notice! I hated him!

"Stop ... Shut up ... My head is spinning ... I feel like running away ..." But what am I doing dressed in bed? In fact, on the bed! Above the covers! My head is spinning! I still have my boots on. "No fuck off, what the fuck do you want, today I'm not leaving here!"

"Come on, let's go ...

" Half an hour later I was in the passenger seat with my head throbbing, with him laughing at me as he drove. Maybe the world was a nice place to be the day before, but that morning there was really nothing to laugh about. My head was exploding! What happened last night? I don't remember !

Towards the Mountains.

In the back seat, his dog, that damned dog. He shed fur on everything he touched, even with his eyes. White, thin fur that eluded the aspiration of most modern vacuum cleaners.

Only he could wake me worse than his master, licking my face after licking his balls. I hated him every time he woke me up in my dark blue sleeping bag; especially when I fell asleep.

When I awoke my bag was covered in a thin white fur with slight shades of blue barely visible. The bastard slept on top of me, not on his master's light-colored sleeping bag next to me.

The one who laughs calls himself Trinca; one of the most absurd people you can meet, and since he is absurd, the most absurd things happen with him.

Who among us didn't try to sleep on the beach one summer evening? The evening is beautiful, there's the sound of the sea waves; the moon is so close that it seems it wants to be caressed; the crackle of a small clandestine bonfire mingled chatter, and nearby, faint music coming from a club.

You lie down and think that life is beautiful, that all thoughts can disappear, erased by a single moment like this during the year.

And then you wake up in the morning!

You no longer have hair on your head. In their place is a solid object with a strange shape, like those nonsensical things that kindergarten children create with modeling clay and then try to mold them into a house, car, mom, dad.

You have a face that, if you don't wash it within ten minutes of waking up, you'll lose the use of your eyes forever, as well as losing your original features, wrinkles giving way to crevasses.

And, usually, you're awakened by a guy who's driving a beach garbage cleaner early in the morning.

Bottles, litter, butts, and two assholes with a dog!

He's absurd, but this was once different.

That is, not completely: crevasses, modeling clay on the head, loss of features were where they should be, but I don't get woken up by the beach cleaner.

I'm awakened by a more beautiful noise, no, not the sea ...

Girls !!!!

Many girls, beautiful girls. Dozens of girls around us, in our sleeping bags, even around the dog.

I wake up my friend. He looks around opening his mouth in amazement.

We tell ourselves ... "We're in heaven! ..."

And a an off-screen voice ...
"No, you're not in heaven! These are selections for Miss Italia, you two have to get the fuck out of here "

After a few episodes like this, you too would have hopped in that car and headed towards the mountains. With a headache, with him laughing, the dog in back, and just like me, wouldn't you have even asked ..."Where in the Mountains? "

We walk. Every weekend he invents a new trail to walk, a new lodge to drink wine.

He was born for the mountains. Not me!

But he made me love it, because he knows how to wait!
Step by step he taught me how to walk slowly, pause to drink from a stream, to fasten the tightest boots, to eat a little honey or chocolate. Step by step he waited for me and my step became more and more secure.

We've always arrived at a set goal. Alone, maybe it would take two hours, with me it would take four, but he always came with me.

Except once!

That time he decided to climb a 3400 meter peak.
Valle d'Aosta. I don't know the name, I don't remember it.
He, I and his mongrel dog had slept in a tent.

Ball-licking-face alarm clock. Breakfast, and away ... we walk.

As we climb the path becomes more unstable. I no longer hear my sicure footsteps. He's convinced, I'm not! He realizes it, slows down even more. Everything gets steeper. It seems to me that we've lost the main trail. The mongrel dog, who's called Diego, looks at me, looks at his master and seems frightened too. He stops! I stop!

This time I'm not going forward. I'm scared! My friend reassures me. I ask if he'll let me have a moment alone and he does. He's goes on ahead.

The return journey is quieter than usual. He talks to me, laughs, but I'm absorbed in my thoughts.

The week after, for the only time, I decide where to go!

Back to the top!

I'm calm. Step by step. Slowly.

We stop to tighten the laces. Slowly.
And again step by step.
The legs are tired, but they're warm.
I'm not afraid.
My friend can wait for me, he walks near me.
We chat and observe nature becoming more and more lunar.
His dog is with us, he's not afraid.
We get to the summit!

There, we meet two people, a young man and an old man.
We eat and drink wine with them. I'll never know their names, but we had reached the same summit and the same mountain had allowed us to. The elderly person passes a cigarette. We smoke silently ...

... And then we go down ...

On the way back, still in the lunar area, we meet a man. Stops! He asks us how much further! His pace is slower than mine but steady, his eyes are determined. He'll also reach the top.
He's over seventy years old!

Now Trinca has moved away, lives near the ocean. It's a beautiful place with a lot of wind.

A couple of hours by plane separate us and we never talk to each other, there's no need.

Once a year, sometimes every two or three, I hear the doorbell ring.
No notice and no timetable. It always takes me a few seconds to realize that someone's ringing ...Just enough time to hear him scream ...

"Will you open up or not? It's me !"

... he knows how to wait!

I have a sister. She, reluctantly, has me as a brother.

While I continue undeterred to fill the shopping carts with beer and chips and sometimes with some chocolates for the Red Cross nurse on duty, she's already finished filling the diaper cart twice. She has two children, a husband, and a dog.

If the dog dies, she'll choose an identical one of the same breed. If I go twice on vacation to the same place I suffer from the phases of the moon; she blames the phases of the moon if she doesn't always go to the same place on vacation.

My sister was a thief! She was still in elementary school and was already stealing my collection of colored erasers and passing them off to her friends as her own. And she would have never told me, I had to get a tip from Ilenia to find out.

And then my sister purposely hit-and-run vehicles! She managed to mangle the bodywork of two cars and a scooter on the very first spin; at least thats what's left to understand for posterity. If she has, in the meantime, run over someone and hid the body in detergent drums, we don't know. And, we don't know what threats Ilenia received after having squealed about the tires ...
... Hasn't spoken again!

And, if you start observing my sister for a week in a row, you'll also witness the exact minute in which she will tie her shoes to go pick up her daughter from kindergarten; where and when she'll get gasoline, how she'll fold the receipt and you'll also notice when she'll glance at some handsome boy; after twenty years with the same man!

... and that man notices it, but laughs and pretends nothing has happened.

My sister is my sister! The brother is the only anomalous variable to a life under control.

But my sister is also a mother and, as a mother, she was afraid for her son because of another thing that happened out of her control.

Hospital.

She's sitting on the side wall, while her son is sitting near the corridor. It's a very common and very normal hospital waiting room on a very normal day of the week. There is a fixed channel television, you can't adjust the volume or change the channel. She doesn't get up to go to the bar because she risks arguing with someone one who could come next, the one who'll surely try to steal her turn. She listens to the normal comments of normal people while she waits and for someone to complain ...

... And if anyone complains, my sister's in the middle of it!

Then suddenly the mood changes. Something happens and everyone falls silent. They're no longer looking ahead, they're looking ...

He's got handcuffs! There are many agents. They're accompanying him to make the visit quickly, almost running. They must pass in front of everyone, it's the procedure. Everyone begins to be afraid, it's the custom.

The man has handcuffs only on his hands, not his feet. My sister is afraid, afraid that he might kick, that he might hit her son ... and if there are so many guards, that man is dangerous! That man looks at her, looks at her son ...

... And she's afraid.

It all happens very fast.

One guard remains outside, all the other agents enter with the man.

She'll tell us about it at dinner on Saturday night. This we have in common, every Saturday evening we have dinner with our parents. Then, she, her husband and children go home ...
... and I go ...

Home? Obviously not?

No, I don't go out like before. Noooo, I said no! I don't drink like I used to. I did get drunk many times as a young man though. There were times after drinking that I don't remember. There were times when I was sick afterwards. There were times ... That everything spun round ... And no ... I'll never drink again in my life ... Never again ... Never again ... Until next Saturday. But every time, every time I remember laughing. I was with friends, and we lived in an era in which you also learn to know your limit, the one that made you say, 'when I grow up ...'

... "Enough!" ... here's to the next glass.

I was also learning about the limits of my body, my mind, my control. Having been involved in combat sports for many years has taught me a lot, especially respect for the opponent, and the punches ... Punches are only thrown in the ring. If someone in a club provokes me, it doesn't come to blows. I'm strong, I have control over the fists and the mind. Yes, I raise my voice. I insult, but I don't raise my hands.

After the age of eighteen I threw only one punch outside the ring.

And that was one punch too many.

I was not drunk, on the contrary, I was totally lucid. Then I saw a friend throwing punches at all the hands resting on the bar in a club. He was really drunk and hurt, and hurting everyone. Everyone tried to tell him to stop, but he kept going.

Then he comes at me; crushes my hand on the counter full-force with his fist; the fingers with which I play ached, but everything was still under control; then he turns to her, and hurts her too, and then control ... I wake him up by pouring beer on him! I ask him to follow me, and outside the club I throw a single punch. He

doesn't stagger, he's very strong, he could probably even hurt me
a badly if he wanted to. But he doesn't want to. He got punched
from a friend who never punches anyone. He understands. He
goes back in and apologizes. We're still friends today. But it was
still one punch too many in my personal journey, after ten years
with boxing gloves.

The guy speaking to me hasn't thrown too many punches!
He's the same age as me but much bigger than me, much fitter
than me, and much taller than me. Over six feet, with two
hundred and fifty pounds of muscle. A former boxer. Boxed for
fifteen years.

It's the cook!

You have to imagine the contrast of this man, tall, big, full of
tattoos, shaved head, who then makes you taste the sweets he
has baked. He's always been a cook; it's his passion.
He managed to turn his passion into a job, and he's good at it.
His first restaurant was followed by others, some international.
He's very good at business and they've always done very well.
And like any self-respecting cook, while cooking with white
wine...

No !

He didn't have the drinking habit..

He knows his body, his mind and even his fists very well.
He's in control. Unlike me, he didn't get too drunk as a young
man. He always wanted to drink and make as few mistakes as
possible. He's a professional. But not knowing his limit he loses
control twice; two times too many ...

No ! Our cook doesn't throw punches.

Our cook laughs; laughs too much and does it with those he
shouldn't. In the right place, the wrong blue lights come at the
wrong time. He doesn't remember the day after. The next day is
the one that turns everything around ... Never again, never
again ... But in the meantime his name is noted a first time and

then also a second time. Always the same blue lights, and he laughs, he doesn't understand, he doesn't remember ...

The next day he's lucid and a different person and those with the blue lights notice it. They point this out. He's just a kid who didn't understand the limit. He hadn't learned it. But meanwhile the name had been marked again.

As there is in every life, there's one day, the one day that you can't not laugh when things go badly for you. The one who does nothing in life and never risks anything ... One day someone worthless laughs in your face. And one day you slap him. Not a punch, a single slap.

And for a slap the cook ends up with a prison sentence.

No punch, and less drunk than me!

He's a cook. He also begins to also cook inside, in that world where the walls are closed with bars. Where there are a lot of bad eggs, some less bad, and those who haven't understood if they're bad ... In addition to a one over six feet, two-hundred fifty pounds who got three years for getting drunk twice and a slap.

He is respected. He respects guards, inmates, educators. No problem with anyone. Cook, wait and do his time. Three seemingly endless years, being a cook inside, and not outside in his restaurants.

After a year, he feels something's wrong. His arm feels like stone. He can't open his hand. Tendinitis. The prison is not equipped, he needs to go to the emergency room. He has to go to the hospital.

They load him in a very narrow space, at least for a person weighing two-hundred fifty pounds, and over six feet. They drive silently to the entrance of this building. He falls down... ... And can't walk! He's stunned, and the guards ... The guards scold him. And to a man weighing two-hundred fifty pounds, muscular, and over six feet ... There are eight guards!

He is stunned by the large space. Inside everything has a logic. The distance of the walls. Colors. The lights. Everything has a precise shape, a shape you get used to too quickly. And when the sliding doors open ...

A woman moves her frightened elderly mother. He's huge, he's dangerous ... ... and he looks scary.

And he looks afraid ...He cannot walk as he walked before.
He feels like his uncle, the one with ALS. Several times he placed his foot on ground that was not as close as it seemed, dangling conspicuously. And the agents have to hurry ...
And he no longer has his bearings ...And people look at him ...

The agents know the route to the emergency room by heart, but he has never been there. By instinct he turns left and they pull him right.

They arrive in the emergency waiting room; he feels observed, judged, and people turn away. They have to hurry, there are nine who have to hurry.

It's a scary thing to watch eight officers running with a big bad man in the middle, and as soon as he tries to look at whoever observes him, they lower their eyes in fear. And he just has tendonitis

...He's the cook!

They skip the whole queue as usual. One guard stands outside, the others inside with him.

The normality of the doctor and the nurse, who attaches an IV, seem extraordinary things to him compared to what he saw before. He, a forty-two-year-old professional, feels pampered.

He'll stay on that bed for two hours, and in those two hours he'll talk about recipes and cooking with a guard. Then the screen is removed ...

And this time he knows what awaits him. Again, the same path.

He focuses on that mental corridor trying to avoid looking around too much. Trying to avoid getting stunned again, disoriented looking at those wide, boundless spaces.

Without the known border of prison walls, colors and lights.

But when he senses the same looks on him again, this time he turns around. This time he tries to look at those eyes. He has two drunks and a slap to serve ... nothing more.

Re-enter the tight space.
Return to silence.
He's very sad.
Now he knows what awaits him inside ...
But he no longer recognizes what awaits him outside!

He shakes my hand vigorously. He's a former boxer weighing two-hundred fifty pounds and over six feet. He's the same age as me but much fitter. I met him when he made me taste his desserts. He's happy to see me again.

Today he has no sweets to offer me and he apologizes for the smell of fried food. He was cooking.

We greet each other with respect ...

Him, drunk two times and a slap ...

Me, drunk many times and a punch!

- Track 12

I am very focused. I'm the man more 'ohm' than any Zen man that exists. I'm ready, yes, I feel ready to meet her. She warned many times and, I mean, you just need to tell me once, right?

Elena, was my fiancée for five years. I don't understand how she did it. Even my parents don't understand. Not even her own. Maybe not even her. The fact is that she has been my fiancée for five years.

Are we alike? No ! Do we have three million interests in common? No ! But somehow five years obviously worked, up to the fifth year.

She also managed to convince me to get a black cat. No, I don't want any cats, I want my independence, when I'm traveling as much as I do and then ... And then the following week I was grumbling on the highway, and on the way back, a black cat the size of a cup of coffee was purring in her hands while I drove without grumbling. He gave her first purrs to her.

Don't try to talk to her in the morning when she punches you directly in the face, especially if she hasn't slept well. And she's such a light sleeper, that she even hears the movement of mites twenty kilometers away, so she never sleeps well.

So, you should never talk to her in the morning. All clear?

Elena was my girlfriend for five years.
And my girlfriend who has much to recommended herself, this time she's not joking. There's this new American friend of hers; they have been friendly for weeks now; she cares for her lot. The time has come to introduce her to me ...
... With her boyfriend!

She warns me. He's a bit peculiar! But I'm the most ohm Zen man that exists, I mean, just tell me once, right?

We drive an hour and a half for this meeting. I'm really ready. You know me, you know that if I'm really ready I'm really ready, right?

We park, we head towards the meeting point which is in the area where they live ... and they arrive an hour late! We're on time despite an hour and a half by car. They arrive an hour late and smiling as if nothing had happened. One hour.

Motherfuckingsonofabitch ...No! Well no! I'm still focused. You all underestimate me. Elena also underestimated me. But this time I won't grumble even under torture. An hour late? It can happen right?

We set out. My girlfriend next to her American friend,
behind me and him two meters away.

He's a normal person. A very normal person who smiles even after an hour delay. NOOOOOOO ...

I was saying. A very normal person. Normal dress. In a normal tone of voice. Of those people you're introduced to that leave no particular impression. An insignificant dude. But the day isn't for us, it's for the girls. We're both aware of it; that's okay.

We pass in front of someone playing a sax in the street.
He asks me if it is true that I play, he'd heard from his girlfriend.
I'm about to open my mouth to answer when a monologue begins
about himself and the fact that he plays and about the music and
about ... and there is no comma, no semicolon; a three-point ...
or even just two of suspension..
I don't know how to interrupt him and somehow try to talk too. A
motormouth. A flood of words placed side by side without any
pause in which to slip into.

It was as if he were speaking for the sake of listening to himself.
And he spoke, he spoke; my god how he blabbed.
And I mean, he was talking about music, not chicory plantations.
He was talking about a wonderful topic, which I love, but ...
... me too ... Please ... I can speak ... I'm drowning ...

Help!!!!

Ohmmmmm ... Focus ...Ohmmmmm...

The two girls turn around. "Would you like a hot chocolate?"

Semicolon;

We sit in this old town bar, very nice, very intimate.

The two girls talk, and my five-year-old girlfriend talks with her
American friend with her back to me. No eye contact.

I am alone with the friend of the Boney M spilling rivers of
Babylon words. Without instructions ...

He asks me if, being from that city, I know that man, a shepherd.
That particular man of God. He lets me open my mouth, and this
time I manage to say ... YES ...

And the floodgates open again.

Faith, religion, sins, God, vocation, good, evil, scriptures, psalms,
churches, non-churches, priests, Catholics, evangelicals,
testimonies, impositions, God, religion, read, understand,
interpret, faithful .... blaaaaaaaaaa, blaaaaaaaaaa.

I turn off my ears. Bypass! I observe him, but I don't follow him anymore. I try to understand how such a person can not understand that if I wanted to have a hot chocolate with a radio I wouldn't have driven an hour and a half, plus with an smiling imbecile arriving an hour late.

How can he fail to notice that my eyes look more at the wall behind him than his eyes. How can he manage to bore me so much, despite talking about things that interest me so much. Before I put him on Mute he was talking about all the things I shared. Everything. But can we insert a comma? Can I talk too?

About forty minutes pass. Forty minutes with a motormouth. Only those who have tried can understand what I am talking about.

Zen is murdered.

A little more ohms, but just a little. I'm trying to preserve it.

I raise a hand. I stop him!

"Excuse me a moment ..."and I turn to my girlfriend, who turns around and looks me in the eye and understands everything ..."Elena ... don't we have to go to the cinema in 10 minutes?" She nods, following the game. I turn to him. "Sorry, you were saying?"

And he understands that I exist ... He asks me ... He finally asks me ... "Ah, I wanted to know what you think ..."

Ohmmmmm .... shit.

"I think if you had been my friend I would have told you to fuck off! But you're not my friend, so I didn't! " comma,

Elena can't believe her ears. Neither do I. I didn't think I could say such direct words. But at least they were aimed at his ears, I wasn't talking to myself.

He replies with ..."Well, if what I said is not useful to you, it could have been useful to others in this bar ..."

"Nah ! I think they would have told you to fuck off too "

Period.

Elena, was my fiancée for five years. I don't understand how she did it. Even my parents don't understand. Not even her own. Maybe not even her. The fact is that she was my fiancée for five years.

Her American friend had been with him for only three months. She still didn't speak Italian well. But the next day she suddenly managed to learn how to write very well, saying that she would never visit her again, because her boyfriend was false and an cynical!

Well, fuck off!

The alarm. One with comics, the Tic Tac hands and the two cowbells. A low and narrow rectangular one, with the liquid crystal display. One that projects the time on the walls. One you set on mobile phones with nightingale songs of love. One that turns on with your favorite radio station. Whatever sound you choose to sweeten the pill, is always the alarm!

... and the alarm clock is hated!

It's overbearing! Without warning we're interrupted from slumber and dreams. It forces us to get up.

We regret that extra hour spent with friends the night before, that extra half glass of wine, that extra cuddle, that extra TV episode. We're sorry.

As we try to wake up the mind, body, hand, fingers to ward off hell, flashing images of traffic, noise, colleagues, classmates, classwork, meetings, take the kids to school, remember to take out the garbage have already arrived. Until a second before they were dreams, and now ...It's too early !

I get up, I go to the bathroom, I hate everything, I hate everyone. I don't look in the mirror, not yet. I leave the bathroom and go to the kitchen. I fumble with the only thing that can interest me in the world as soon as I wake up: my coffee pot. Water, coffee, fire.

I go back to the bathroom, I hate the mirror, I brush my teeth, I go back to the kitchen and ...How come she's the only one here? Where is he?

He spent the night out again!

I open the balcony door, it's early morning. The sun, too, has not yet brushed his teeth completely. The school bus hasn't passed yet, the bell is half an hour away. To my right I see my neighbor who, dressed like the little man from the Permaflex commercial, is smoking his first cigarette of the day. I don't know what his name is, I've only recently moved here, I don't care, now the cat is gone.

I look left towards the woods, look right towards the road, and scream ...PAAAAHHHZOOOOOOOL ... PAAAAHHHZOOOOOOOL ...

After a few seconds, my black cat, Puzzle, comes out from who knows where and scurries up to me on the balcony. He starts to rub on my legs. The neighbor stands with the cigarette between his two fingers in midair, and with amazement he asks me ... "You call your cat, and he listens to you? "

Wish it was my cat! I'm his. He's called Puzzle because he's missing a piece of his tail. We don't know why, the legend has it that his mother, was a Carthusian cat, but in reality he has no resemblance to a Carthusian. It's a black cat in all respects. The father must have been one of those who clung to cars as they crossed the street. The first time he saw me he climbed onto my back, and stayed there. I didn't want him, but the following week, to the jubilation of my girlfriend, or rather former girlfriend, I went back to get him and he climbed on my back.

In the morning, while the coffee is percolating, he and Caramel, the cat I found in the house who became his sister by right, tear apart a few bags of cat food.

It was easy to call him Puzzle. I loved doing puzzles as a kid. I started like all children with those 4 piece puzzles. The ones you finish immediately and then remain forever in the toy bin forgotten. Then I switched to the 20 ones, the ones that ended up in the bin after two goes of five minutes each. My parents understand, and finally here comes my first ... 100! This is starting to be a proper obsession; but why do they write puzzles on the package? Later the 500 arrives, and the first trouble. As a genius I find myself inept. I start again from the frame, the border is easy, but after ... What's this white piece with a slightly gray edge, is it the snow or the cloud near the mountain? And what is this black piece of the horse? Is it the neck, the tail, the hoof or the mane? Somehow I finish, after days of total concentration and ... And a piece is missing! That missing piece will twist your balls more than bad grades at school. That missing piece that you searched for under the sofa, behind the furniture, inside shoes, in the newspaper basket ... Missing forever!

I read all this awareness in her daughter's eyes as I offer her a puzzle as a gift; the same youthful passion. I'm at my friend's house, who been a father twice. I've known him for many years, and I have also known his wife for many years.

But before we get to her: Pushers!

There are those with a thin shape and those with a plump shape. The thin ones are in for pounds. The plump ones are in to shed pounds. They're young. Our protagonist is 14 years old and 240 pounds of softness. He's in a room with four other accomplices.

Clinic! The corridors are low, white ceilings and dark blue lights ... gloomy! The thin and the plump are divided; also on the other side is his best friend, 5 foot and 88 pounds.

There are few points of contact: the school or the church.

There's no rivalry between them. They're fighting the same war. Skinny and plump are both in the same shit!

The difference is that the thin ones are smothered with kindness, the fat ones are deprived of it. For them fruit, small chicken legs but the thin ones also eat badly, poorly seasoned things, bland dishes without color or flavor.

The skinny are in solidarity with the fat, and my friend now knows several pushers to rely on: forkfuls of pasta are passed into paper napkins, as well as spinach pies. Some pushers do it out of pity, some assholes gets paid.

But for both of them there is a mirage, a word, a myth:
the hut!

The hut was a small kiosk in the middle of nowhere that opened its doors only on Saturdays and Sundays, when the thin and fat family members visited their children. In the kiosk there was everything: coffee, chips, sweets, junk of all kinds.

If you were fat and tried to approach, they caught you right away, but if you were a skinny fourteen year old, with that particular jacket, with that particular way of doing things, maybe you could get the:

BIG BUBBLE !!!!!!

And then you were no longer terribly skinny and now with grown-up problems. No ! You were a superhero that the Japanese were worth nothing in comparison, and that's it!

At night there was control, there was patrol, and every now and then you could hear phrases like AUYT% UIODIKSKN $ J & DIN, which also woke up the dead in the nearby cemetery.

After six months, my plump friend returns home without the 120 pounds he had on the first leg; but the desire to eat does not decrease. This desire does not come from genetics. The family back round is optimal, the family is united, but there are problems, big problems for those who were delicate and sensitive. The grandmother is not self-sufficient and the mother is increasingly stressed and tired. The father is never there, he works from midnight to noon on normal days, and from 6pm until noon the next day on weekends: baker. He's so tired that he falls asleep while eating, and sometimes even with a hot cup of coffee in hand. He finds his escape valve in food, and after a few years, in the church. The parents have always gone to church, and attending church was a normal part of life for him.

He begins to study the Bible and play music during worship. In church he meets his wife. They get married.

... and after a short time she has second thoughts.

He gets up very early every morning and prays. Seeking solutions, and help.

"I met her in church, what the fuck do I still have to do? " What happened to the 'until death do you part?' I can't be divorced ... A divorcee for religion is ... Worse, much worse than any rail thin guy or any of society's roly polies.

Divorce.

A divorcee for religion is failure.

He hates all women except his mother.

The church, his church, supports him, but ... It waffles a little. The doubt. The blame for a divorce. Wasn't there still a chance? Even if his wife is gone, and she also left the church, are we sure that he has really tried everything? Till death do us part ... She swore it!

He isolates himself. He tries to stem the anger but he can't. A year and a half goes by, he's no longer in love, but he's all darkness, darker than the arm when he was being drawn seven times a day. And he's so grim he never notices her.

She wasn't part of his church yet, she was approaching gingerly. The second or third time you participate is for a marriage announcement. She doesn't like him at all, he's not her type, yet that voice keeps telling her: "He's mine! What's he doing with that one there? ". He's my what? The one who is getting married?

Some time goes by and this thought keeps coming back to her, and she chases him away cruelly ... He's married, she's now part of the church, it's a bad thought. Besides, he's not even her type. And then he also lives far away.

Then he divorces.

The thought "He is mine!" haunts her. She decides to ask God for confirmation, the only one in whom she has truly begun to believe: "Let's do this, if what I keep hearing is really true, prove it to me, let him get closer to where I live".

Shortly after, before worship, he tells friends that he has moved home, that he has moved to that county that ... She remains speechless. You see that ...

" No ! It can't be. He doesn't even see me ".

"Let's make it harder; I like motorcycles. If that's what you want, if that's him, let him come to church by motorcycle "

At work he runs into a colleague, who stops him.
He offers him his used motorcycle. He doesn't need it anymore
and ...And then he arrives by motorcycle. But no ! In any case
no ... He doesn't see me.

And no, he didn't see her! Blonde, with a weird nose and a harpy
look, he likes those brunettes like Cucinotta ...

But while he's working he sees her photo appear, it materializes
on the computer screen, two seconds before disappearing.
He doesn't understand what's going on, but whatever it is, he
doesn't like it. It is annoying, what's the one he saw in church
doing before his eyes. He doesn't like her, go, shoo!

After some time he invites all the kids from church for a pizza at
his house.

That day's a disaster in everyone's life, glitches everywhere, only
two people show up: a friend of his and the harpy face.
After pizza the three remain chatting, and at a certain point his
friend starts snoring. He falls asleep without warning. They move
closer so as not to wake him, and while they are close, she puts
her hand on his belly ... On his flabby belly. For the first time he
doesn't feel any discomfort ... And he starts to ...

They start dating, but there is still a big problem to overcome.
Divorce in their religion. They are devoted but ...
He's divorced, and a second marriage is not possible.
They confide in each other, and are advised to keep a low profile,
not to expose themselves yet. Let's see how Lord deals with it.

Some understand and start cheering for the two ...
Others understand and ... He's divorced!

And the Lord?

They go on retreat with the whole church, they can't hug each other, hold hands, get noticed. He's nervous. It's as if he had received the Big Bubble package, but he couldn't unwrap it. They invent a lottery to pass the time, where the prizes at stake are used clothes or those basement funds that even the basement no longer wants.

They are all there:
those who are cheering for;
those who not cheering for;
those who know nothing.

She pulls out a ticket and wins a package. She throws it away in front of everyone.

It's a videotape, a used VHS.
The title is:

"The second wife",

Starring Cucinotta.

Some start laughing, others start crying. It's God's final response. In their church, subsequently, re-marriage is evaluated on a case by case basis; the church is made up of people, and people inevitably make mistakes.

This is the best story in the life of my pudgy friend, who isn't even very pudgy anymore. He now no longer needs to eat so much.

The Second Wife does not look like Cucinotta; if we're honest, not even the first one was like her. Among other things, it was the first owner of the motorcycle who said this in the book ...

All the pieces of the puzzle fall into place, those with a slim shape, and those with a plump shape. Even if I started to tell about the setting, seventy thousand people around him at the Circus Maximus in Rome, it would never be as important as his greatest love story. I see this awareness in him, the same awareness in his daughter's eyes as I offer her the gift ...And a piece is missing! That piece that's missing and ... It will be missing forever ...

The piece missing from my cat's tail ...

... And maybe it was mine.

Instead, I am his.

- Track 4 -

We've already studied, observed, stalked.

Wherever she was, wherever I was, I saw her face appear among the photos of friendships in common; or acquaintances? Or just potential blue thumbs up?

I knew how she smiled, who she went out with, what she loved to do, how she wrote, and also how she felt when she was a little down; I had also heard her before, there were videos of her singing, joking, playing, acting for the blue thumbs with a friend.

Out of five senses I already had two, **sight** and **hearing**, obtained with less effort than a channel change with the remote control.

"Friends" but only in the sense to have received a virtual greeting on my birthday, a pat on the back that is always virtual in a sad moment, access to those photos and videos that only her "friends" could see.

We appeared on each other's home screen. It was enough! It's always been enough for us!

I go to a summer party, in the kind of country I love. The volunteers of the Community Associations provide beer on tap, taking half an hour to change a keg, and grill chops with white aprons, not really even white when bought; those in the country without a job either drink, eat or complain; then there are those from the chorus that can't wait for the party to start for their moment of popularity: call the police because the volume is too high.

I recognize her friend near the stage. And she is next to her. While I'm in the line I haven't decided yet whether to defend myself or attack; protected by shield and sword in the same hand, my beer held at half height in front of me, I approach. We smile at each other with music and smells in the air.

It was all very spontaneous. We chatted as if we had known each other for a long time, as if I had already been to her house, and she had flipped through two or three vacation albums with me. I've always hated when friends forced holiday albums on me, etc. Better a hornet stinging my knees. But now I browse curiously, now that I can decide when to do it, and from the comfort of my sofa, alone, without an audio guide.

I meet her on several occasions. Live music venues. It amazes me. She comes by herself! In my city I don't think there are women who go out alone to clubs in the evening, or maybe I just don't notice. She does it without problems. Says hello to everyone without problems. She laughs and jokes and sometimes drinks without problems.

She comes by herself ... but won't be that way for long!

She's cute.

I make her a proposal. It's not too difficult to accept. My place?

She arrives wearing a nice perfume. **Smell!** The only things lacking is touch, taste and I've hit a home run.

She has a confident gaze, clear ideas. She's younger than me, but she looks older than she is. She realizes I'm shy, she reads it in my face. She smiles at me. She could be on stage. She knows her stuff.

I take the initiative. We talk about Love.

Finally she turns very red. It almost manages to make me blush too, but here my experience wins. I'm almost twenty years older than her, I've cornered her.

Love. Absurd stuff.

It was all very spontaneous. We smile with our perfumes swirling around. We chat as if we've known each other for a long time.

My proposal wasn't difficult to accept. My place?

She's a virgin.

It's saved for the right person.

Filthy minds! I knew it when I invited her!!!

It was all very spontaneous. We smiled with our scents swirling around … Those of the dinner we cooked together.

We ate for three. The **taste** was gone.

The time came to say goodbye. A kiss on the cheek. It's the **touch**…

Score!

Either black or white. I've always been told it's wrong to be black or white. I've always been told that the truth is somewhere in the middle, somewhere in the gray area. But gray sucks to me.

When one is small, sooner or later he receives them as a gift: Marker pens. They come in giant packages, and there are many, They're fantastic, they're very colorful. With them, yes, with them I'll show you how good I am, how I can change the canons of art.

And then you remove the cap from the first marker, usually the one with the most unusual color, the one that is a little water-colored and a little air-colored; a cross between blue, green and ...and water. Five minutes after opening the marker, you don't know why, color materializes even on our fingertips. Always !
And it's completely different from what we've seen on its plastic cap. Like perfumes, which change according to the skin you spray them on, the color of the marker changes once it gets between our fingers. If they haven't forgotten to buy the ... wait ... and usually they forget ... we try with our fingers already tattooed with color even the ... mmm ... those ...

Come on you understood, those where you fill in the figures with colors. The kind that the people who design them today still haven't understood that the contour lines are too thin. Could you make them a little wider??? It's impossible to stay inside them. There will always, always, always be a bloody red smudge; an apple with a slightly square side, a bee with ruined wings that would crash a second after take off, just like my paper airplanes. And then, excuse me ...But do you think we're all as smart as you are? We're four years old, we're not architects. How the hell do we color Snow White and the Seven Dwarfs with the door and the plant and the leaves and the buttons and the step and also the bird on the plant, if the outlines have such fine lines that as soon as I barely try to place the tip of the felt-tip pen on it, I've already painted the same color as Snow White's arm, the door jamb, and even the bird?

How the hell do we color the smurfs holding hands with the clouds, the sky and then the pond? I mean, can't you buy me the blue? Later my mother doesn't understand why I no longer play with markers. Doesn't understand. It's not very much fun to play with just the colors I have left: brown, that dark green that you can't really look at, that pink that isn't pink, and gray! And gray sucks for me.

I'm either black or white! Either I like it, or it makes me sick. Like Guinness! What? What's Guinness? That black, Irish beer that has a foam as thick as cream, and that when you drink it for the first time you feel like you're drinking something bitter and strange, and definitely not beer. Either you love it, or it makes you sick. There's nothing in between.

And I'm lazy sometimes.
I am so lazy.
I'm really lazier than you can imagine any lazy person.
I'm lazy even lazy to be lazy.
And I'm lazy and bored ...very...

And sometimes I want to get very bored.
I don't feel like it, do you understand?
I don't feel like doing absolutely anything.
I don't feel like reading.
I don't feel like writing.
I don't want to work.
I don't feel like going out.
I don't want to wash my hair.
I don't want to talk.
I don't feel like doing anything.
I don't want to think.
I don't want to...

Nothing !

This is my black, and I love my black!

There are periods in my life where in the eyes of those who don't know me well, I = hyperactive = Extremely white.

I'm here in the morning, but this afternoon I can't because I'm there, but I have to hurry because in the evening they are waiting for me to work ...And then I write, and then I play, and then I teach, and then I work, and then I love, and then set the alarm, and then I play, and then I go out too, and then I laugh, and then I don't know if I can, and then I love, and then I work, and then I never sleep.

"But how do you do all these things?" Wrong question!
You should ask me ... "But why are you always running?"
I always run because the sooner I finish and the sooner I can go back to being ...Lazy!

I run like crazy = White

To get to ...I don't feel like doing anything = Black

And black is a blessing. My guilt-free black is one of the best sensations a man can experience. I need to be bored.
My leisure becomes a pastime. My idleness becomes pampering myself. And my idleness, once it's allowed my head to go completely blank ...Become ideas. And ideas become notes, and notes become phone calls, e-mails, filling up the car, arriving, writing, teaching ...I run! My black is a blessing. Without my black I couldn't do white, think it ... Dream it. My white wouldn't exist without my fantastic and very black creative idleness!

And if someone wants to convince me it's all wrong?
What's wrong with not wanting to do anything?
What if that someone maybe has a strong influence on me?
What if that someone is perhaps particularly intelligent?
So intelligent that he can persuade masses with his talk.
What if that someone's a great thinker and makes me feel stupid?

Does it make me understand that I can't get there with my head?

Where would my white be if I didn't do my own thing?
Where would my black be?

Simple, there wouldn't be anything!
It would all be gray.
Gray sucks!

And she's disgust with gray.
Neither dead nor alive ... Apathetic.

She's a captive in a marriage that she imagined to be different.
She didn't believe in fairy tales, for heaven's sake, she was a very
rational person. After several years of dating, you either break up
or get married. There are no flames of passion, but she wants
tranquility. That's fine with her. She marries him ...And she didn't
realize that ...

Law ... He was the law.
No !
She's not beaten.
No !
She's not isolated.
She becomes...
Manipulated!

Everything must be under his control.
She has no freedom.
She's in marriage, and marriage is ...
His.
Her work is also his.
He can manipulate everything.
And then wash, wash away everything.
You touched the handle, wash your hands and also the handle.
But no. Nobody gets to go out with friends without her husband.
And...
Each step is checked, followed.
And that's okay with her.

That's okay with her!

She gets up in the morning. She feels balanced.

Goes to work. Works well. She's always worked well.

Clients think she's sick. She's gray. But they don't tell her.
They're clients and she's an important professional.
Besides, she doesn't confide easily, it's not fair. She's married...
With her husband.

Can she handle all of this? Sure! The worst that can happen is
what one can no longer endure.

And there are no money problems, as there often are with those
who do a job like hers.

At home she tries to rest, but she can't. Must wash. She has to
clean up. She has to cook. She cannot stand still. Standing still is
a waste of time. If she tries? Blame and feelings of guilt ...
And she doesn't want guilt.

Gastritis arrives. Colitis arrives.

And she goes on.

White, white, white and more white.
Never stops. If she tries, guilt.

He's with her as soon as she wakes up; at work; while driving;
while shopping; while cooking; when washing; when you go to
sleep ...And always controlling everything. Controlling
everything!!!

The worst thing is she can't stand him anymore, and she bears it.
He's smart. He's very polite and formal, very formal. He can speak
well and sometimes even tries to be nice. In everyone's eyes they
are a perfect match. He's the man. She's the freak ...

... and it goes on!

She's free. She's very free. She is free to decide nothing.
She has no time to think. He's always with her to lay down the
law. In her ordinary imprisonment there is security.

Routine and the habit of sadness also create security.

It was enough for her to be calm.

Unique little moments ... Tiny moments of black ... When she shakes the tablecloth on the balcony. Thirty seconds.

In those moments she's alone ... And looks at the sky.

Thirty seconds a day. It's her only black stain!

Months go by and she shakes the tablecloth. Years go by... Many years. Many more years than it takes for a child to be born, grow up, go to middle school and even have the first kiss. And one day ... ... and finally ... ... the apple falls on Newton's head.

She feels her stomach tighten as he enters the house. She get's a headache. She goes and shakes the tablecloth and looks at the starry sky ... "If anyone is up there ... Extraterrestrials or God ... Will you come get me or ... ???"

No beam of light ... ...

or decide!

Waiting. Still waiting a long time. She's not strong enough yet but she's alive now. It's not yet time but now she's alive. She's hesitant, but she is alive.

And while alive she makes plans ... Two years!

And while alive she glimpses what she is looking for ... "Oh my God, that's what I've always wanted"

For her now everything is very clear: she wants her home, and her's only. It's just like that. No rent.

Two years of tunneling for the perfect escape. Slowly, methodically, inch by inch.

He doesn't suspect anything.

Then one day ...
The day...

She's no longer at home. Not that one.

She had everything planned.
Even that he would try to block accounts.
Even that he would call relatives, friends, lawyers, psychologists.
Even that he would have begged her to stay.
Even that he would have threatened her.
Even that he would have belittled her.
Even that he would still try to manipulate her with his reasoning.

But she's now free. Responsible and free to decide and not to decide. Free in the black!

Start doing things without expectations.
Start doing things of no importance.
She starts shopping on her own, and is surprised at how wonderful it is to do it.
Start listening to the silences.
Start choosing to do nothing.
She begins to choose to be bored, without conditioning.
She looks at the void for an hour, even two, and is happily aware of it. And in the void come ideas ...
Starts painting.
Starts singing.
Starts dancing.
... and go to the gym too

And she changes her mind, she often changes her mind, and every time she changes it she feels wiser.
If she changed her mind, it wasn't the right way.

And she does not judge, she never judges anyone who has been judged so much. "Why didn't you do it before?"; how many times will you be asked ...But you have to be in the same situation to understand!

She doesn't want to advise anyone.
She learned that in order to make the decisions she had to listen

only to herself by silencing all the voices around. She no longer has internal voices.

And now she dreams, oh yes she dreams ...

Her paintings will be sold at disproportionate prices ...

Before extinction she wants to do a striptease ...

And before extinction ...

Dream of a Man!

We've always been told that it's wrong to be either black or white. We've always been told that the truth is in the middle, somewhere in the gray area. But gray sucks to me. You too...

and...

I love Guinness.

- Track 7 -

I was going fifteen miles an hour. First, second and I didn't put the third. Behind me there was a column of headlights all going fifteen miles per hour. Someone honked the horn. I didn't listen. I smiled, I was happy. What I was transporting was very important, but even if I had hit a pothole, going fifteen miles an hour wouldn't have damaged it.

I've never seen one like this before. I was used to different weights, but the length was always the same. There was the modern one that you could hold in one hand, open the door and load into the car. The one you held with one hand you used to play your ass off in the rehearsal room. There was one that required two hands because the engineers who had conceived it must have had a background in construction. But never so long.

I arrive on Saturday afternoon, as usual, after crossing the freeway, road and path. Scattered houses; backstreet has never had a more appropriate name. As soon as I get out of the car I feel something's wrong. I look in the back seat. It's there, so nobody can ... The others have already arrived. I open the door. I hesitate to enter.

He's seated. He's dressed exactly like last week. Bad. But he's as bright as the sun. He doesn't raise his hands but instead nods his head towards the open door not yet closed. He smiles at me, beckons me to come closer. I'm a bit scared.

The year before, hearing something that I didn't recognize before entering the rehearsal room meant that someone had taken my place. But in this case my guitarist is smiling at me, not another keyboard player. There's no new face with a sarcastic smile, a winner without having competed.

I come closer. It had three gilded pedals, embedded in a custom-
made cabinet. Above the cabinet a very long series of keys, and
above the keys an elegant door that hid built-in speakers.

I had never seen a piano before. I didn't know it had eighty-eight
keys instead of sixty-one on a electric keyboard, nor that the first
key was not a C but an A. And I'd never even seen a digital piano;
what my friend was playing.

The drummer, bassist, and singer all smile at me.
I don't understand what's going on.

"It's for you !"

The guitarist had made a phone call the week before.
He knew a guy that had eighty-eight keys collecting dust.
In the meantime the guy was already playing with something else.
The guitarist asked for a loan. Indefinitely.

He moves over, makes me sit on the stool. This also agitates me. I
was used to playing badly while standing, but a piano. A piano
cannot be raised with one hand while making an ass of oneself. A
piano is respected, and it's played seated.

I was 19!

After a couple of months the group broke up, but the friendship
did not. The guitarist invites me to take the jewel home with me.

To make it fit in my car, we had to lower everything possible and
keep the trunk half closed with a rope. Path, road and then
freeway. I was going fifteen miles an hour. Behind there was a
column of headlights going fifteen miles an hour. Someone
honked the horn. I didn't listen to them. I would have another
instrument to play.

Many years pass. Meanwhile the loaner is returned to the man
and the dust. Groups, projects, dreams, are born ... They die.
The passion for notes was born late but it's still not dead.
With passion, more and more modern instruments take the place
of the previous ones.

In a moment of enormous economic difficulties, when I no longer
had even a musical dream to hold onto, I decide to sell the only
61 keys I have left. I've had it for many years and perhaps it's the
only technological object that really gave me soul by playing it. It
hurts me but I can't make it through the month. A prospective
buyer arrives, and notices some doodles on the keys. It was my
personalization. The tattoo that I don't have on my skin I did on
my keyboard. Sounds good. He likes it ... but those doodles.
No sale.

Somehow I get to the end of the month.

Even today, Miss doodles is the only one that remains among the
more modern ones. She has lasted. She deserves to be with me.

A little more time passes and I notice an advertisement.
From the photos, it looks like ... Yes ... It's that model ... It's
her. ...That eighty–eight someone has for sale. I'm going to see
her.

I try it, load it in my car and take it home. Highway, expressway,
road. On the way back, I drive the car at the same speed as the
first time.

I place it in my study. Three years gathering dust. The sound was
no longer as modern as the latest generation digital pianos.
When playing it there were no vibrations that I felt with that
drummer, that bassist, that singer ... and that guitarist, who

looked at me and smiled. It wasn't her. It wasn't the same. It was
just a slightly dated technological box.

I place an ad with her photo with a brief description.
A person answers me who wants to come and see her.

Mother and son arrive. A surprise Christmas gift for the husband.
He's only starting now: they say it's never too late.

I try to help them load the eighty-eight keys. It doesn't fit in the
car. They don't give up. On the roof! Ropes, and more ropes ...
"Is it moving?" "No, but go slow !!!"

You can't imagine the light they had in their eyes ...
And you can't even imagine mine ...
As I watched that car drive away ...

Going fifteen miles an hour!

Grand Canyon. I came here to sleep.

The day before the exam I had sixteen books to review. Sixteen books to study took up the entire kitchen table. I was about to open the first one, but then I decided. What's done is done, I load them in the car. I drive slowly, the dirt road with holes so deep that only cars that cost very little or that cost a lot can survive. And with my tiny economy car here I am. I get out, spread a blanket, unload and distribute all the books from the car. Sixteen books. I glance to the right towards the plain from which I come, a glance to the left towards the mountains, and a glance at the parallel road, another at the end; far away. I lay down on those hundreds of pages ... ... and I sleep.

The next day I see panicked faces that scan random pages taken from sixteen random books. Not me. What's done is done. I was relaxed, and had slept well that afternoon and at night. And I passed the exam.

Coming back here today isn't easy ... ... for the climb! Today I live in the hills.

I live in one of those places where if you wanted to build a flat football field, you'd first have to plow down some mountains. The houses are comfortable, the view is fantastic, but even just to go to the vegetable garden or the lawn behind the house, you have to brave a few meters in altitude.

When you look out on the balcony you see the intrepid cyclists tackle that climb that was Pantani's, the one that made history, the one where the chain fell off, he lost ground, but then recovered. And when you watch intrepid cyclists, you're happy to

be on a balcony with a beer your hand. You feel like crying and
sweating just looking at them. On Sundays the shouting starts
early in the morning, when groups of friends or families decide to
brave the famous walk towards the sanctuary, the Sanctuary of
Oropa. After a while you get used to all this, to the difference in
height in the garden, to the tears of cyclists, to the chatter on
Sundays. But you never get used to what you see a couple of
times a year:

The Transhumance.

It's a time versus time show. Everything stops. They all stop.
There's no more traffic lights, pedestrian crossings, overtaking
lanes and right of way. The road is theirs! Shepherds, donkeys,
dogs, and hundreds of sheep. They cross the city to change the
pastures, towards the plains for the winter season, towards the
hills and mountains for the summer season.

The sheep pass between cars that have stopped. The sound of
cowbells replaces that of motors and scooters. And they, the
shepherds, proudly parade with their army. The dogs also seem
to have an attitude when they cross town.

After they have crossed the city, they climb hairpin turns that
sometimes are a stage of the Giro d'Italia. But when the tour of
Italy changes stage it does so to applause. When the shepherd
changes stage he walks towards other silences.

I live in the middle of that stage, and twice a year I observe this
army from my front door, once as it goes down and once as it
goes up.

I studied that 'book' for three months every day.
I took notes, looked at photos, read stories, and also realized that
there are codes; codes that will never belong to me, but that I will

respect. The codes of looks and many silences. The codes of small gestures that only other pastors could understand.

I won't look for the moment of shearing. That must remain their moment only, the moment in which they meet after a long while to help each other, and finally chat a bit. I will not look for them when they choose cowbells, and I wouldn't even dream of marching with them during the transhumance. And I will not look for them on the paths that only they know by heart, following traces of black balls.

No. I don't want to disturb them.

I would simply like to observe them for a few days, and during some other routine days of the year. The normal ones where the sheep are hungry for grass, and where the grass is sometimes difficult to find in the snow. Normal ones where they cross streams. Normal ones where they cut, scrape, disinfect and sew. The normal ones where the dogs sink their fangs, where the sheep get the mange. The normal ones near the rice fields, where the lambs are put in sacks and loaded onto donkeys. Those days where the umbrella is opened, and those where one can observe for hours. Those where one crosses stony ground, and those where one chooses the dog from the litter. Those where one rests, and those where one talks to the farmer: one whose envied a little for the stability ... The other that envies a little for the movement. Normal ones where there's fog, loneliness, isolation, and where there is silence.

Normal ones.

And I would be silent.

But I can't.

It seems that, like the army, the shepherds also have diplomats and spies. I contact those who know a shepherd, we talk to each other on the phone, and of course ...There's no problem; and then he disappears. And then a friend. Call that one, who knows the another. And no. He's not there anymore .. Ok, but he must have gone somewhere else, right? And then the young one, the one who's not the son of shepherds but has decided to lead this life. It will be easy with the young one, right? I'm silent, I don't ask questions, I don't write but I observe. But I'm left with only silence. ... And no shepherd. And while someone sees them here, another one sees them there.

I studied that book for three months every day. I understood that there are codes, and I want to respect those codes. It doesn't work if I spot a flock, park the car, and walk to it. It wouldn't work. The silence of a shepherd would be mute, it would not be a living silence. Everything has to be done with a lot of respect. I can't go into the general's tent alone. I have to be introduced. But when someone tries to tiptoe in, I was always left out.

I give up. Rightly so. I am nothing but a stranger to a cleaner world where a man still understands animals, and animals understand the man with a whistle. And I don't even know how to whistle. I was presumptuous. Observe and try to understand someone who does not go on vacation, who does not have a day off. I, who as soon as I have two cents, look for a restaurant by the sea.

Tell this to someone who chooses a life of sacrifice and solitude, and if he earns something, he uses it to buy himself an extra field, a field where the flock can taste the delicious grass of home.

But 365 fields would be needed.

How can I watch, observe, understand and write about someone who has made a choice of solitude, without leaving him alone?

I give up. Rightly so.

But I don't give up on meeting those who took those photos that I studied for months. Who has had the opportunity to tiptoe into the tent, and stay there for four years. I look for him, I find him, he answers immediately. A phone number, an address, one afternoon.

I walk into an office that seems out of time. They ask me to wait, a slight delay. I observe in silence. Photographs on the walls, paintings and books exude the smell of history. The colors are warm ones of wood, warm tones of black and white from the past, the real ones, what modern cameras can imitate but never attain. There are pens and paper. There are hard covers that are worth more than many books on the market. And on the shelves I read a title ... Up there, the last ones. There's one about the memories and the hopes, the pains and the joys, the sadness and the happiness of the "last" left to guard a treasure of millenary traditions. My "Hunger for Grass" is next to it ...

And I understand!

Giuseppe arrives. He looks me straight in the eye, smiles at me, and gives me a strong, very strong handshake; light years away from the grasp of those soft hands that slither as you try to gauge the personality. He asks me to sit down. We speak slowly, very slowly
As we speak, I feel my thoughts. They are moving slowly, very slowly, like the weather in that room. I don't remember the world I left out anymore.

I'm with my grandmother talking about Africa, and I'm in the

meadow with my cousin looking for worms ...I'm among the
yellow dragonflies in search of a red one, and I'm hugging the
trunk of a walnut tree ... My mouth is full of wild cherries, and I
spit the pits on my friend ...I have red mercurochrome on my
knee, and I'm picking the shit out of my shoe with a stick ...I'm
chewing the berries of the cucca grass, and I'm counting for hide
and seek ...

And as we speak softly she explains to me that all those books
are just a thread of a button, that you'll never see the whole shirt.

I get it !

And use the phone ...

It wasn't my plan to meet him. Not him. After a few days
Giuseppe raises the tent for the general. I tiptoe in. He looks at
me. He looks at me as if I were a black sheep ...And I talk to him.

I have to stay focused, the dialect is very hard, but I understand.
The humor is also in code, but I understand.

He recently met his another friend, the one from the book, but he
wasn't very well. He doesn't leave the house much anymore. But
he still has 300 sheep and a dog ...No, shepherds today are no
longer what they used to be. Once you were born to live that life
and that was it. The life of one of the oldest professions in the
world.

While talking to him every now and then he looks at me.
I'm one who could viewed as a boy. Polite, well dressed, with
crazy hair. I certainly can't understand much ...
But I'm sticking to the codes.

They talk more and more, and a lot of things I can't grasp.
I don't take notes, I don't write ... I observe ...It's enough for me
to just be next to the general.

Then they stop. Giuseppe asks me what I would like to know.

What would I like to know? I feel that I can never be and know enough. Not even if I asked a thousand questions would I have all the answers.

I only have one question ...

"Why does one want to be alone so much?"

The general watches me, and his eyes cross mine, straight, without deviation. He tells me in a dialect that's not difficult to understand ...

"You are alone while eating soup, and if you're not focused while using the spoon, you scoop the plate, not the soup. The sheep and dogs, after a while, settle down on their own. You have to stop dancing around it, after a while things are done by themselves ...
And... don't worry ... The book also writes itself "

I hadn't talked about a book ... and not even to Giuseppe!

The caregiver arrives, kindly asks us to say goodbye ...

Salute his blessed mind ... he still has 300 sheep and a dog ...

Coming back here today is not easy. As soon as I opened the front door I saw the descent, and I realized that it would get a lot colder before arriving on the plain.

In the city I started pedaling, and I did it for about twenty kilometers. Then uphill, and on the left that road with holes so deep that only cars that cost very little or others that cost a lot can overcome ...Or a mountain bike.

I support the bike against a tree. I'm approaching the edge of the Grand Canyon, that's what I've always called it.

A look to the right towards the plain from where I came, a look to the left towards the mountains, where I arrive. I lie down on the ground. I rest, a difficult return awaits me. In the distance I hear

shots. There are military exercises. And I think of the
general. ...Who often came here with his army in winter.

I live in the middle of that stage of the Giro d'Italia.
On the asphalt there are still white slogans of the fans.
I try to give myself mental references when I'm uphill:
comes up to that tree, then later up to that road sign.
But after a while my legs beg for shorter and shorter landmarks ...
I reach that house, and then in the middle of the house, and then
to the end of the same house. But I go on. You can't go down.
Sheep don't go on vacation. I go slowly, but I go on.

The last few meters I can't take it anymore, but I notice that a
neighbor is watching me from the balcony and I find energy
where none existed ...

... and I sit up proudly

I'll finish the book tomorrow ...

... The book also writes itself ... He's right.

Today my phone rings ...

Next week I will live a few days, the normal ones ...

... I will be silent.

- Track 8 -

Do you know how long it took them to cut the bottom of the
basketball net? The regular kind, where you make a basket, you
go under, pick up the ball, and start playing right away.
It took them twenty years, in fact, twenty-one.

Before, they just kept a ladder behind the basket, and every time
someone made a basket: wait a minute ... go up ... retrieve the
ball ... go down ... and start playing again. Twenty-one years.
They invented basketball in 1891, and cut the net in 1912.

And they weren't kindergarten children, they were adults, who
among players, referees, fans and even friends and relatives were
tending that ladder. They waited, and not even while they waited
did the idea occur to them. And it was easy. It was that easy.
It was so easy and obvious ... After! I'll bet anything, that if we
had been there in 1911, watching a basketball game, we would
have done something else while someone else took care of the
ladder, except thinking about cutting the net. At least we went to
the bathroom! But someone did think of it, and now we take it for
granted.

Some things are obvious if we see them every day.
We hear about them every day. But in reality, they're not quite so
obvious. And when my neighbor called me, I knew what awaited
me. A very difficult period lay ahead.

My neighbor absolutely wanted to buy a computer and asked me
if I could teach him how to use it. And my neighbor was over
eighty! And he couldn't leave the house. He was confined to his
kitchen, his bedroom and bathroom. And everything he knew
about computers, he had seen on television.

I provide some photos, explain what I think it would be suitable
to buy. He puts the money in my hand, and says: "You do it". His
wife Anna Maria mumbles ... He mumbles at her ...
And I buy the computer.

A good laptop suitable for photos, videos, games, and in the
future, if he wants, to go on the internet. But let's not worry
about that now. ...

We discard the packaging. He asks me the first, legitimate
question. Why aren't there any instructions?

Yeah, how come there aren't any instructions? How can I explain
it to him? He always carefully read all the instructions of what he
bought.

If I buy a car stereo, there are instructions.
If I buy a TV, there are instructions.
Why aren't there instructions?
Like how to turn off the computer?

No! Stop! That button is for turning it on, not for turning it off!

Wait a minute I'll show you ...
I move the mouse and ...
And wait a minute ... Sorry ...

These two buttons. The one on the right, pretend it's broken for
now. The one on the left is for ....Sorry again. This is a monitor. It
will be the displ ... it's like a television where you see what you're
doing. These letters are those of a slightly more modern
typewriter. This flat thing is for moving that arrow. You see?
Exactly ... Hehehe ... You want white wine? Yes, thank you ...
Cheers ...Then you'll see what that arrow is for ... And then....

And calmly. Very calm. A lot concentration, his and mine ...
He learned to use the computer. And quickly.
So fast that after two months ...We take on the internet.

And Anna Maria shaking her head ... And they make me laugh so
much while they mumble ...

Are you sure?

All right!

We start looking for an offer. A subscription arrives. And ... No ...
wait ... Noooo .... Go back. No, that's advertising ...No... The mail
is not inside the computer. Yes, I understand that you see it here
but ... Yes, so ... An attachment is ... I mean imagine that ...

And after a while I become comatose...

The days pass. He does crossword puzzles, a passion he'll never
abandon; but if he doesn't remember one, he starts laughing ...
Wikipedia is really the bomb! Yup ... And I laugh too ... While he
pours me a glass of white wine!

And after a while I don't hear from him anymore ... I changed
houses and ...And every now and then I go to visit Anna Maria
who would really love to still have him grumbling next to her ...

I'd like to explain these things to the guy who talks to those two
elders in the phone department. He's a salesman and they simply
asked for information about a cell phone. He's showing off his
knowledge rather than giving explanations. He's scaring them,
and he looks like he's happy doing it. And the more it scares
them the more they ask questions. And they feel stupid not
knowing about the obvious things, like 3G or Wi-Fi, or streaming.
They want a phone, and suddenly they're stupid.

I'd like to explain these things to the guy who's talking ... But I avoid it ... I go to the two elderly people who have given up in the meantime. They left without a phone. They're sad. I give the genius a piece of my mind on the way out, and they smile at me under their lenses.

Genius of phones ... Its people like you that would still have a closed basketball net.

Do you know how many take a piss while waiting for the ladder?

I finish the yogurt, 'Y' wasn't in my alphabet yet,
I go into the living room, I move some of the grown-up
newspapers, I move my mom's newspapers, and there's mine.
Yellow cover. Red writing in the middle. Mickey Mouse.

I take my routine scolding from momma ...
"You haven't finished eating yet ..."
I'm in the bathroom with my pants down.
A wonderful sound of electric heater that just hearing
it I already smelled the heat.

And atop my legs the new Mickey Mouse. Six years !
And the new Mickey Mouse arrived every week.

It wasn't two or three days after I bought it that I had already
finished it. I was only in the middle of first grade. I started
immediately with the smaller stories. Not the first story nor the
last. Those were longer. I immediately moved on to the stories in
between, those with the characters I liked best, those with Donald
Duck, Scrooge and Huey, Dewey and Louie. I also liked it when
cousin Gladstone came to make Donald Duck feel even more
unlucky than he was. Furthermore, I liked Grandma Duck. And
Daisy Duck. There was also Fethry Duck. And then if there was
Gyro Gearloose, I always had something to laugh about.

Before moving on to the long stories, the more challenging ones,
I then started reading the short stories of the book's protagonist.
Mickey himself. Well, yes, Pluto, Goofy, Minni ... Peg-Leg Pete
too ...I never enjoyed the adventures of Super Goof as much as
the stories of Duckburg.

When I was leafing through the toy advertisements for boys and girls, I always struggled with this word ...Barbi E.
Why is there E in the end? If you say Barbi, why do they write Barbie? Grownups are just weird.

In elementary school the teacher said I was not as clever as my classmates. And the more she said it, the more I wanted to be as good as my classmates. I didn't study history that I didn't like, or grammar either. I studied Mickey Mouse every week, and I learned to read a lot. And in the third grade, came the inserts to learn how to play chess. I didn't have a chess set or anyone who was interested in playing chess with me. So I took some cork and a knife; I cut my finger and I still have the scar in my left middle finger to remind me. I made myself some very ugly chess pieces that only looked like chess pieces to me. But reading the figures that explained L for the knight, and the diagonal for the bishop, by eight years of age I knew how to play chess against myself. And I understood all the rules ... Alone. But for the teacher, I wasn't as good as my classmates.

And I wasn't even good when I finished before my teammates. When she gave us the number exercises I always finished first. They seemed very easy to me. They were very easy. And then, in that case, she didn't even tell my momma that I was good. No, she called her to report. She told her I finished too fast and disturbed the class. In short, I was really nice to the teacher, and when one is lucky, he keeps the same teacher for five years. But in the fifth I realized that maybe I wasn't slower. I wasn't even faster in many things. But I certainly knew how to read well, I understood what I was reading. I had a scar on my middle that the others didn't have.

And I also understood who was the first person to whom it was dedicated ... especially when she slapped my most unfortunate partner.

We all knew who was being beaten at home.
The one who couldn't study and had to work already.
We all knew it. And she knew it too.
But she had thrown the slap anyway.
And he was crying. And we couldn't do anything.

She was our judge and executioner.
Our judge was wrong. The executioner was bad!

Over the years I've continued to read. I've had both 'readers block' and the better known writer's block. But sooner or later the roadblock is lifted, and I start over. I consume books and I consume them thanks to Mickey Mouses that over the years have accumulated in my bedroom. Not enough to end up in those record-breaking photos, the ones where children are sitting in the midst of hundreds of comics and next to them their dad and mum with columns of comics as tall as they are. No, not that many, but my parents allowed me a few hundred.

I don't consume books because of the slaps.

And not even the child I meet years later consumes books thanks to those who slapped him. He's more or less my age.
"Could I have another coffee?" ... he asks me between one cigarette after another on the terrace.

He was terrified. His desk mate had just returned with a chalk-smeared forehead. In addition to the slap? he had also seen his head squashed against the blackboard.

First grade. And then the teacher calls him. And he's classified as "slow", along with eight other "slow" out of a class of thirty.

And the teacher was also a priest ...

If the teacher is also a priest says so, then he's certainly slow.
He trembles ... He's at the blackboard ...
Questions: the first answer is right ...
The second he's bit confused between the plus and equals and ...
... And he didn't see him swing.

And that slap doesn't hurt. It hurts him to receive it from
someone other than his dad. Dad can! But the teacher and the
priest can't!

And his lucid anger hurts. It makes him understand that he can
not return the slap. And even if he could, he wouldn't have had
enough strength. "I would like to make you understand what
you're doing to me! "

And while he beats him ... He fondles her ...
And their everything, school, religion ...
... all becomes one big fuck you.

My friend and the other seven lose the desire to try.
The desire to make the effort passes away.

And the beatings continue.

One day the father receives a letter from the teacher.
A real letter, white envelope, with the edge glued with a tongue
lick. He opens it. Looks at the son. Tears it up! He prefers to have
him lose the year by changing schools, rather than having him
return home with chalk on his forehead. He will never know what
was written in that letter. His father told him that a seven-year-
old boy certainly didn't deserve those words.

And maybe not even one on trial for murder.

Nor a hero.

A masked hero.
Like The Duck Avenger.

When he's on a mission, no one knows who's under that mask.
Only others like him. They can't have a curtain call on stage.
And they can't expect applause. When the mission is
accomplished the curtain is still closed. When someone opens it
Clark Kent has taken over for Superman.

Imagine winning a race and not being able to tell anyone.
Imagine having foiled an attack and not being able to tell anyone.
Imagine bullets, boots, flames, blood, mud, snow, tears, sweat,
thirst, hunger, and death ... And not being able to tell anyone.
Can you really imagine it? You, me, have our photos, our smiles,
our victories, on every particle of the existing web?
Can you, can I really imagine it ???

He is one of the "slow" ones, do you remember? He is so slow that
when a problem arises he can't even think about it. He must
outrun his fear. Look it in the eye, and smash it in the face.

Tremble, sure. He trembles, but he knows what to do.
He was trained for this. He knows exactly what to do, where,
when, and with what timing. After the A there's B ... and after the
B there's always C. Discipline, coolness, and orders. And orders
are never discussed.

His mind runs on tracks that are close but don't touch.
That of life, that of death. That of man, and that of the machine.
The machine does not think. It acts.

The machine has levers, and depending on the situation you have
to operate one lever or the other. And if you are operating the
other one it is because you were ordered to. You do not argue ...
You act ... Quick ... Always Quick ...And if you were slow ... It

would be death! The death ! Your death, the death of your
comrades ... The death of civilians. And you are trained because
death is approaching ... but it doesn't affect you. Death flows
nearby. You respect it. And it doesn't touch you!

And then he takes off the mask.
People don't know who they are and what they do.
He's Donald Duck again.
The loser next to the cool Gladstone.
That even his uncle takes into account.
And he can't speak.
Can't take selfies.
He doesn't want to take selfies.
And he asks me for more coffee.

I know him but I don't know him.
He can't tell me everything, and if he feels like it ...
He doesn't come, and I don't make him come!
He has to be alone. He has to be alone for some time before he
can ignore it. All heroes must be alone after each victory.
The only trophy they have must be kept to themselves.
It's called Duty!

And when there is no longer any fear to overcome.
No fear to face.
No duty to respect.
Then he trembles ... He trembles again ...
Because that time he didn't see it leave ...
And it doesn't have to happen again.
Because even if he doesn't see it leave this time ...
There could be some death.

And then enough! The Duck Avenger is finished!
The Duck Avenger has to take off his mask and not put it on
anymore. End of all missions. But people only know Donald Duck.

And even the end cannot be told.
And a tear flows, and this one is slow.

He has to be alone. He has to be alone for some time before he
can pretend nothing has happened.

And he was alone even when he entered the fog.
The compass didn't work.
There was no one to give orders.
No one to give directions.
He didn't know where to go and started running.
All logic had collapsed. Everything he knew crumbled.
It was like filling a garbage bag with pieces of bone that shatter
and fall apart.
And without stability ...
He fell apart too.

And in the fog ...
In the fog, what's inside you ...
There are no heroes.

And the fog hurts. In the fog there are monsters.
And he had to face those monsters alone.
But the more he was left alone, the more those monsters
multiplied. And the more intense the fog became, the more it
hurt. Like his lucid anger. The kind that makes him understand
that he can't slap it. And even if he could, he wouldn't have had
enough strength.

"I would like to make you understand what you are doing to me!"

Depression?
Call it what you want ...

He calls it Fog.

We're on the terrace. He lights another cigarette up and doesn't try to offer me one. I'm in one of those stages where I'm a confirmed Non-Smoker and he knows it ...Until the next one ... From 0 to 30 without crossing the street.

He plays with my cat, trys to smile at me ...and looks at his hands. Strong hands. Hands that saved lives.

And then he saw that it could be normal.
That he could learn a normal job.
With normal people.
Who treat him as bit of a loser.
A little Donald Duck.
They cannot know.
They don't have to know.

Fear...

He repaired the compass himself and figured out which way to go.

Must run faster ...

Look it in the eye ...

And smash it in the face!

"...And don't ever call me a hero again or I'll kick your ass!"

Grown-ups are just weird.

ACT TWO

They looked at me

Behold, I am sending you out like sheep among wolves
Matthew 10:16

- Track 5 -

He screwed me again. How is it possible that he always manages to screw with me? Besides, I mean, we were just talking, right? I said how I'd do it, I didn't say he was wrong. A normal exchange of views, me and ... Damn, him again ... Trinca

The question is really simple.

He doesn't want to baptize his little son because he's not a believer, period. Any objections? No! ... and I agree.

With him you walk for hours and while you walk you talk for hours. One reflects for hours. But don't think of us as two wise men who philosophize about the mountains. We, between one sentence and the next, tell each other to go to hell, burst into hearty laughter, and shoot enough bullshit for a couple of screwball movies. We're talking about the baptism of a small child and that's it. The rest is too deep for two minds like ours.

I simply expressed a sacrosanct opinion, moreover starting from two very different assumptions from those in which my partner has: I'm a believer ... and I have no children ... For me the choice is easy. I would baptize my son ... I don't have one anyway!

But in addition to religious reasons I would baptize him because ..

His son would soon go to school with other children. Most of the other children, as is the tradition of our flock, would have already been baptized.

I don't have to tell you that Trinca isn't part the flock, but he listens to me.

With baptism, they would issue the 'card and the first stamps' to practice catechism with the other children. Preparation for first communion (imagine if I used this word with him) I always detested catechism as a child, and it did not bring me closer to religion, or to God; other experiences have done that.

But we're not talking about that either. We're just two very simple minds, chatting between a belch and a fart.

After a few years, with the card and two stamps, baptism, and first communion, children who are now teenagers can accept confirmation. And then later, if they want to get married in church, they must have all three of these stamps, at least in the Catholic church ... Our flock.

Trinca was baptized. He also made his First Communion.
He also had his confirmation. If were honest, he also worked as a carabiniere (Italian Paramilitary Police) in a previous life, but that's another story.

I tell him ...

"You have chosen whether to believe or not ... As an adult
do you want your child to be able to do the same thing?
In the meantime, let him experience same environment as you
did, and the same environment as the other children ...

Because when they do activities like catechism (but I hated it, right???), he might be excluded and start off on the wrong foot ...

Very sketchy reasoning and has as much in common with religion as an eggplant with Nutella ...But we're not two wise men. We don't even have a problem with that.

And as we walk we completely change the subject.

We get where we need to be ... We eat ... We drink ...
we burp ... we go back down ... we laugh ... we each take a shit ...
and then each of us returns to his own home.

Until the next day!

The phone rings. I answer. It's him.

The conversation was ...

"Perino, you convinced me ... I'll baptize my son ... But I want a
friar to do it ... And you can find the friar for me ... Oh, and you
can also be my godfather!"

... And then hung up!

He screwed me again ...

You understand that I didn't ... I mean ... I just wanted to chat ...
And now ... Where the hell do I find a friar?

And what friar ??? I mean ... Do you have any idea how many types
of friars there are?

No?

Augustinians, Dominicans, Canossians, Carmelites, Capuchins,
Doctrinaries, Franciscans, Franciscans of the Immaculate
Conception, Lebanese Missionaries of all kinds, Jesuits, Hermits,
Legionaries of Christ, Oblates of various saints, Servants of the
Paraclete (???), Rogationists (???), etc. etc. etc.

I don't know about you but this word convinced me ... Capuchins!
I'll googled it ... I'm not joking ... ... and I found him.

The Capuchin Friar.

Mail. He answers me by calling the number I put in the email. He's not sure he's understood.. After a while, despite himself, he realized he had understood correctly. It's a mission impossible for him too ... But he accepts.

The day of the baptism he visits me first, he wants to know who found him on Google, and has a few hours to chat. He tells me about his vocation. He acts like a talent scout regarding my potential. He gives up after ten minutes. We have a drop of wine. We smoke a cigarette. He tells me he plays music. He tells me about his ex–girlfriend, the one who understood that he was born to be a man of God. She accompanied him towards the vows. And then we smile and hug ... We are two brothers.

We go to Trinca's ... his son ... mountains and meadows ... all relatives were invited to hold hands. It was more beautiful than the most beautiful of our plans ...and I became a godfather. But not before I received a good slap on the back of the head with a warning ... "And see that you behave well".

The Capuchin friar found on Google ...

But if we want to be honest, he also worked as a carabiniere in a previous life ...

But that's another story.

I can't stand it anymore. I can't stand his voice anymore.
I can't even stand that of others anymore, but **his**.
His is just killing me.

It's four in the morning, and I'm dragging my legs from a stage, a large square and a van. Or rather, what a few hours ago was a stage, what tomorrow will remain a large square, and a van.

We're taking down lights and speakers. The only speaker we couldn't turn off was that of his voice. It's one of those with the volume POT (potentiometer) a bit fried; it no longer rises gradually by rotating it clockwise. It remains fixed for half of the dynamic range, and when it reaches the other half, it shoots you full force in the face.

Born as POT, grown up a On/Off switch.

His voice is only On.

I'm dead tired and pissed off. I feel like a pouting child; I don't want to load this van; it wasn't in the plans; it wasn't in the deal, and not after today ...

after today ...

The fastest way to go deaf overnight? Easy: do stage sound for a heavy metal band. What is the stage sound engineer? I'll explain it to you right away.

You know when you go to those big village festivals ...
where there is always some band playing ...

and you're in line for your third round of beer, they give you in a clear plastic cup, slightly bigger than a small one but definitely smaller than an a medium ...
But why do they make you pay as if it were an medium?

There you are! There's the stage, and on the stage the band is playing, that's easy. In front of the stage you'll then see a very recognizable professional figure: the sound engineer!

He's the one who tends to be badly dressed, sitting on a stool, next to a thing, all knobs and buttons that the most cultured people recognize as a mixer. And while the group plays, and you're happy because in the meantime you've had five beers, he remains with a neutral expression.

In front there may be singer–songwriters, punk and folk groups with accordion solos, stormy blues or Salento choral ... Neutral expression ...

Press a button, turn up the volume, check a level ...
Zero emotions ...Except when someone brings him a beer.

Then...There are concerts gigs, those in stadiums that to get tickets you have sell you soul to the devil. In these gigs there are sound engineers, versus sound engineers, people involved in the hauling of wood and even men who deliver pizzas, next to the drummer.

The slightly larger concerts, where everyone knows what to do, are great. Not like smaller concerts ...Let's say medium.

Yes, here I am, I'm the one on the stage in the right corner, the one who is waving at you. Stage engineer in a medium concert, One who's usually thrown away at the end of the concert ...

Used and thrown away like certain razors. You can try to use him for a second concert too, but only after giving him a month's rest to recover his hearing.

It's a motorcycle rally.
The motorcycle rally consists of two fixed things: motorbikes...And those who gather.

Those who gather are divided into groups, types of motorcycles, geographical areas, and so-called ... Colors. Actually divided is the wrong word, because all the motorcycle rallies I've been to always have a lot in common, even between different groups and colors. And contrasts.

Some of those "who gather" are big. Some even look bad. Very bad. And then they hand you a beer while you're in line. They smile. They're very polite. And then, after over indulging for several days, they go, and they leave cleaner than they arrived.

Contrasts. I don't know if that's always the case, maybe I just got lucky.

I don't know all the colors of those "who gather", but I've seen many thanks to music. Dozens and dozens. And every time the contrasts always left me with a smile. A very positive smile.

The "Who gather" at motorcycle rallies need two other things, besides of course the bikes: The beer ... and the volume.

And what guarantees enough volume?

A Heavy Metal group!

Exaaacttllyy...

It's my lucky day. I'm the stage engineer for a Heavy Metal group.

But I haven't told you yet what a stage engineer does. The stage engineer is the one who, before dying, tries to adjust the volume, to the taste of each musician.
The musician on stage, at least in medium concerts, has low, trapezoidal, ugly, dusty, beat-up, faded speakers in front of him ... only for him.

They are commonly called ... Stage monitors!

Each musician has his own, and the singer often has two!

Every musician has power over his monitor. For example, if the drummer's does not want to hear the guitarist because the bastard uses a dirty drumstick as a toothpick, he will not hear the guitarist. Next to Mr. Neutral you'll hear a guitar at an infernal volume, but next to the drummer you'll hear only the bass, the drums ... Look at the stage ... Raise your voice a bit ... And you won't hear the guitar. The bass player's wants a little bit of everything ... And can you raise the speaker a hair? Always. The singer ... Raise the vocal a bit ... I can't hear the vocal ... Raise the vocal a little more ... Ok, perfect ... Do you also want some bass? No ! And as soon as they all play together ... I can't hear the vocal, can you raise the vocal ???

To who do they ask these things, to Mr Neutral? No. The stage sound engineer. The last asshole in the evolution of the human species. The one who doesn't hear the songs, hears the parts of songs taken apart by the monitors.

In the afternoon they warned me who the metal band was. It should have been easy ... Taking insults. The singer was known for insulting anyone; on the radio, on television, at motorway restaurants. The singer was perhaps known precisely because he insulted anyone. And for allowing myself to be insulted they give me a new tool of technology: a tablet. Yes, one of those rectangles you play or read the newspaper on a plane.

And what am I supposed to do with this thing?

Simple! You adjust the volume of the monitors directly next to the musicians ...Directly next to Heavy Metal musicians ... On the main evening ...

Of a motorcycle rally!

Yes ... I deserve a minute of silence.

They arrive ! They start placing their instruments on stage. They look at me like every group looks at a sound stage engineer at an average concert. A cross between "I don't know you" and distain. "I don't know you" is dangerous.

The singer who insults everyone comes next. First they organize the stage, their musicians. Instead of a stage monitor, the drummer has two stacked speakers, which are as tall as a refrigerator.
The bassist and the guitarist have theirs and don't move it, I'll kill you. The singer has two with a tremendously lethal volume potential.

It's time for Mr Neutral ... The real sound engineer ... The one badly dressed and on the stool ... The one with the mixer ...
Go drums, now bass ... bass and drums ... ok guitar ... mic tests ... good. The song comes out well.

We'll be monitors!

I walk up with my fucking tablet and stand next to the drummer. He is thin ... nervous ... and thrashes like a beast on those cans. He starts to unload kick and snare drum rolls, toms, and holy shit it's absurdly loud; while I try to figure out how to stay glued to the ground next to the earthquake he mimes with his mouth: 'louder' again ... and again ... and then he stops ... he's happy.

And one ear is already ringing.

With a whistling ear I go to the bass player, and what does he tell
me? Yeah ... Raise the box ... again ... again ... can't you do it? ...
Raise this speaker .... Then he wants a bit of everything ...
louder ... louder ...And my eyes become slits.

I go to the guitarist. I'm scared. But him. He says, uh..
Okay, it's ok already!

It's okay?

I feel grace circling around me with fragrant flowers ...

But after an instant that grace is slaughtered!

Here comes the singer, the one who insults everyone. He places
himself between the battery and its two very powerful monitors.
He says one word into the microphone and a tile falls down from
the village church. He doesn't even look at me ... I don't exist! He
nods to the other three horsemen of the apocalypse and a song
erupts ...for Mr Neutral and for me ... fittingly ... The apocalypse.

Behind me is the drummer who is pulling down the plaster from
the walls, he has ripped the back of my head open; the bass
player on my right broke my eardrum; on the left I feel absolutely
nothing ... and in front ...front...Turn it the fuck up ... turn up the
vocal ...

And I feel like crying ...It is very loud ...Loouuwwddeerr ...
Loouuwwddeerr ...

I finish crying, the volume intensity, a dynamic range beyond any
indicator of madness that any tablet ever produced ...

Then raise the thumb.

Everything stops ...

And I'm deaf!

and that was not in the agreement ...

I don't live in London or New York. Going out alone there isn't embarrassing. We sit at the counter of a bar, and a guy starts talking to us. Like in the movies, where there's the bartender who wipes glasses in front of two strangers talking to each other, right? But for us, those who go out alone are usually looked at as losers and are inventoried on the shelf as product A or product B.

Product A – Sad lonely and hungry man. Written in red across his forehead it says: Divorcedseparatedwantstofuck.

Some live ones are at twelve o'clock; he continues to turn his head between nine and three, with fleeting looks at two and ten. Checks out any products of the female gender. Tries to make eye contact, which in turn they completely ignore. After a few weeks he leaves the bar undetected, he's probably being treated for a stiff neck. But he comes back!

Product B – Happy lonely and hungry man. Written in red across his forehead it says: Divorcedseparatedwantstofuck.

He's happy, he's perky, he's dressed like a fifteen–year–old with new Nikes on his feet like out of Flashdance. It's a bit flash and also a bit dance. Happy. You must be happy with him. He's happy to meet you. He talks to you as if he has known you for a lifetime. He also introduces himself to those around you, and nudges you in the ribs to point out the female who just passed. He disappears for periods of time. "You know, I met that girl in Milan, who worked abroad, I've been away for a while" ... But he comes back!

I run the risk of ending up being looked at as a tier A or a tier B guy, even if I'm a tier Y. I recently broke up with one that I won't even dedicate a semicolon, and I still haven't figured out what part I'm looking at.

I accept any gig that's offered to me in order to pass minutes, hours, days and time, anything is fine.

But ... This was not expected.

I feel like a pouting child, I don't want to load this van, it wasn't in the plans, it wasn't part of the deal. Not after I nearly went deaf today. And that makes feel me alone ... I can't stand it anymore ... I can't stand his voice anymore ... Why is our Mr Neutral so cheerful?

It's four in the morning, and I'm dragging my legs. And he's been doing it all day too. But he does it with brio even at four in the morning.

I, on the other hand, am dead on arrival. I'm tier Y. But he's not. Besides not being deaf and having a girlfriend, he has something to be happy about because he already has all the sacraments ... only marriage is missing ... Yes ... I said it all... even extreme unction.

At six and a half months, still the womb, she was in a hurry to make her voice heard, and she played in advance. They thought she wouldn't make it ... But they were wrong.

Conjectures swarmed around him. Words I didn't know. Actually no ... one yes ... CP... Communist Par ... ah, isn't that it? Infantile Cerebral Palsy ... ok, sorry! Paraparesis ... (???) Born with encephaly ... Central system inflammation ... Hemiplegic ... etc. etc. I don't want to leaf through medical manuals ...

Not even him!

He's a musician and an engineer, not a scientist.

Will walk like this forever. As a baby he was already limping, the expectations were not rosy. So, physiotherapy. Reaches the standing position. And starts breaking balls.

It's obviously not contagious. It doesn't get any worse than any of the other illnesses. That is, he doesn't have those diseases like sclerosis or ALS (weren't they the same thing?) At worst, as she gets older, he'll limp a little more. And of course, with age he may well end up in a wheelchair. But he has the same odds as any other person, except that if he has voice commands, he'll wreck his wheelchair.

And walking like this, let's say a little strange, he meets his girlfriend ... Actually ... No ... Not walking, but bumping into her ... Against his gastrocnemius muscle. She's a physiotherapist, and he's stopping by for a muscle stretching operation.

You know when you try to touch your toes? If you try every day, it becomes easier and you're more flexible, elastic. In some extreme cases, the elastic can no longer be stretched, and then surgery is necessary. He couldn't put weight on his heel.

She doesn't see him come in but she hears him, which doesn't surprise us as her speaker has a broken volume knob.

She is very shy ... He's not. They talk about music. He's a bassist and plays the type of music she likes.

The word "Friends" replaces that of "Add to friends"

A couple of months go by and very few blue thumbs. No exchange of messages to break the ice. No accelerated two clicks: "Add to friends" on one side, "Confirm" on the other.

It was done!

Then she goes to hear him play without his knowledge, and the next day the first comment on a photo of him on stage.

The first answer. An invitation to lunch.

A first kiss, and for her love arrives at that exact moment.

It's four in the morning, and I'm dragging my legs from a stage, a large square and a van. We're taking down lights and speakers. He's doing the same thing, but he doesn't look like a pouting child like me. When I met him, I asked myself a few questions and gave myself the answers ...I didn't dare ask him.

But today, after many hours together. After the four of the apocalypse came down from the stage smiling and complimented us. To me and him ... Mr Neutral ...

Today I wouldn't ask him any more questions ...

Because I can't stand his voice anymore ...

- Track 10 -

Previous life. I am an electronic technician.
I'm used to traveling for work.
Taking a plane or a car is the exact same thing for me.
The plane landed.
I follow the directions.
Passport control.

I arrived in South America. No ! Not in South America. In the American south. If we really have to say it all all, in South East America. Let's say ... The Apulia of the United States. I speak English, I now my way around. I can't wait to go and retrieve my suitcase, get a rental car to get out of the sterile environment of airports. I want something real after all these hours of flying.

I have an aspect that my colleagues refer to as 'Taliban'. Hair haphazardly arranged hair on the head; prominent nose; dark eyes. But I don't, I don't see myself being described as a Taliban. I look more ... A Turk; yeah ... I look like a Turk. But my passport is Italian. My father's Italian. My mother is from South East Italy, Apulia, the Original one. And my name and surname on my passport are undoubtedly Italian.

My turn comes to immigration control and the officer asks me: "Uaiuaiiih ???" I roll my eyes! I didn't understand anything at all. Yet I am English ... I apologize: "Sorry?" "Uaiiuaairh?"

Either this guy ate a ping pong ball and it went sideways, or during the flight they ripped a temporal lobe from me while I was sleeping. I ask if he can repeat it more slowly.

He looks at me like I'm a Taliban. A real Taliban asshole!

UAIIIII DE FACCCC IUUUU ARRRRR IIIIIIRRRRR ???? Why the fuck you are here ... AHHHHHH ...

Now I understand ... Why the fuck are you here! I answer feeling like a Taliban in front of a big and pissed off immigration officer. My colleagues were right. He takes my fingerprints. He treats me very badly. After a while, he sends me away brusquely. I go down to get the suitcase. Fittingly I find it smashed with a nice note from the American Border Police that said more or less: "Don't complain and better thank god we let you in!"

A few months later I have to leave for Saudi Arabia. For that occasion, I had to obtain a visa with a photo in a suit and tie. Mandatory. Naturally I don't wear a jacket and tie for the trip, it's deathly hot in Saudi Arabia.

I have a look that my colleagues call ... Taliban. Here I should be treated like one of their own, at least here!

I arrive at passport control. I understand the immigration guy's English very well. I also understand clearly the gestures he makes to a colleague when he invites him to come closer. He doesn't like my hair, but most of all, he doesn't like my earrings. All the other passengers have already passed the check. I stay there.

I'm alone in a place in Saudi Arabia that's not even Saudi Arabia yet. That place in the world that's nothing, the one just before passport control.

They're looking at me as if I'm an American. An American with earrings and a real asshole. I don't say anything. I don't smile, maybe that's the reason. I hope something happens.

After an eternity they decide to let me in, sending me away brusquely ... And they flay my suitcase at the controls.

I arrive in Belarus. I mean, here we're in Europe right? Nobody can take me for a Taliban, much less for an American. I'm italian. I'm an Italian to whom they try to explain how they lost his suitcase, just after passport control. I am an Italian who looks like a Turk. I'm not in Minsk, but I'm in a smaller city that has so many consonants that I have a hard time spelling it.

I go to the hotel restaurant. I feel everyone's eyes on me. Everyone knows I'm not a local. They know it by the way I'm dressed, how I gesticulate on the phone, how I pour myself a beer, and also how I drink it.

I feel alone. I feel damn lonely. I'm being scrutinized by eyes and they're not joyful eyes either. I have no one next to me to gesticulate with.

Another Journey... Turkey. Finally at passport control I do not run in a hurry. The suitcase ... Arrived safe and sound, and no checks.

I take a taxi, a ferry, and arrive in a city on the Asian side. In the evening I go to a place that appears particularly crowded. They block me at the entrance. They speak to me in Turkish. They don't think I'm one of them, they only know Turkish.

I try to explain that I'd just like to have an EFES beer. They tell me No! I can't enter unless I am accompanied by a Turk. There's a racket inside and I'm out with the bouncer. This time I just don't want to be alone.

I come the next evening. I try again. The bouncer smiles. I smile. And with my smile I go back to the hotel without entering.

I come back again the following evening. I have a CD in my hand.
I tell him it's for the DJ. With gestures I make him understand
"Give him the CD to the DJ and I'll go".

The bouncer goes in and I stay in my place ... Outside. He comes
out. Opens the door. He points me to the place and makes a sign
of no. Then he points to the bar and nods yes. He smiles. I smile.
The DJ smiles at me, thanks me ... and I get a drink.

Society is racist. Society has made me feel out of place over and
over again. So many times that I can't tolerate racism!

I already understood this as a child, when I went to the pool with
my cousin Laurent. The son of my father's sister who came from
Africa, but then went to Belgium, and came to visit us in the
summer.

I was trying to get dark with a tan. He, on the other hand, simply
became darker with a tan. But that wasn't the difference. The
difference was that he had hair with different curls than mine.
Cooler ... Tighter.

And so this asshole was more beautiful than me. And the girls
always looked at him and not at me ...

Racists!

We meet in a very sunny house. A place that belongs neither to her or me. It's a meeting that we both want, and whoever organized it for us created a wonderful corner where we can have a chat isolated from the world.

She welcomes me with curious, lively, and slightly sad eyes. We're cheerful, spontaneous and impertinent, like children who meet in kindergarten for the first time. We immediately feel at ease.

Her first daughter had her birthday on the same day as me, 11th of February, the day of Our Lady of Lourdes, Mary. Born 34 years after me.

She tells me this as I adjust the gray blanket over my legs. I'm a bit cold. Not her!

She's originally from Milan. She belongs to one of those 'baùscia' (poseur) families who bring the city to the mountains on weekends. We smile a lot as we talk, but she always has this sad look.

She reminds me of a boy about my age, whom I observed many times when I was also shy in high school. He too had this sad look. I never had the courage to talk to him. Maybe deep down I too had that similar sad look in the mirror.

The bullying period. All my energies were directed at staying alive.

Besides the sad eyes he had a peculiar face, like a bonnet on his head; or so it seemed to me.

I have always been sensitive to slightly sad looks.

They always make me feel bad.

The looks of some elderly people who shop at discount stores.

The looks that some lonely women have with regrowth in their hair.

The looks of some who sell roses to cheerful people in clubs.

I wish I could talk to them; help them to be less sad. But sometimes you just can't. That period was "you can't".

She didn't notice anything, until kindergarten. An extraordinary mother and a teacher who facilitated out her childhood. No particular look, no uncomfortable questions from the other children remain etched in her memory. Nothing. All normal.

"When I started something new, I immediately explained everything, so I didn't have to deal with it anymore. So, I told you, period! "

... gone, no more curiosity!

A bit like Meryl Streep in Silkwood, a worker in a nuclear power plant, when she immediately shows her breasts to a new colleague to avoid future curiosity and distractions. ... and gone, curiosity over!

Her mother has always been a real badass. Her memories make her smile. She recalls an episode and tells me about it with her proud, smiling, and a slightly less sad look.

Stroller, her mom, and they encounter a lady. The woman looks at me and asks her mother: "Madam, why don't you put a bonnet on her? "... ... Madam, why don't you put a bonnet on you ???

This is her mother. The woman she remembers as one who prepared her table but did not cook for her. That did not allow her daughter any shortcuts. She had to walk, she had to make mistakes on her own. She would not accept any experimental surgery for her daughter. At the age of eighteen she can decide.

This was her mother until the year she passed away after 3 years of illness. She passed away when 'baùscia' Meryl Streep was 19 years old. She did not see the harvest after so much sowing.

The first real episode, the first feeling out of place, happens in fifth grade ...She doesn't understand exactly. All she knows is that a friend of hers tells her not to notice. What ... Whom?

He had never felt any such sensation before. Despite the slightly sad eyes, despite the bulky hearing aid. The out of place blossoms for the first time in fifth grade. Perhaps when children begin to discover that they can become adults. When maybe children start discovering they can turn into assholes!

Treacher Collins syndrome, or Franceschetti syndrome, or mandibular–facial dysostosis.

Call it what you like. The auditory pinna does not develop.

The bones of the skull develop abnormally.

There may be cleft lip.

The jaw is poorly developed.

The appearance of the eyes is the most obvious feature: gives a "sad look".

No physical malformation below the neck. None!

Above the neck no mental illness. None!

Her parents could neither foresee or expect it. Nobody in the family had this type of disease. If they had known? The father replies smiling: "Dunno ... You're here ...! "And the daughter mimes the father and his shrug of the shoulders laughing.

If he could have chosen her? He would have said No.

She met her husband at the age of 17, the boy she saw on weekends out of town. His family, friends, don't like him always seeing this lonely girl on weekends; this sad eyed girl.

But love wins. She's 27 when they get married, and they're still together!

"He is kind! "

There have never been any problems inside or outside the home. Physical deformity is not well accepted by society, but in any case, there have never been problems. She's learned to avoid them. She knows the world. She instinctively knows where to put herself when she enters a room, close to certain people or far from others.

"Anyone who has experienced bullying like us, knows which side of the sidewalk to walk! "

From their love two twins are born with assisted fertilization.

Assisted reproduction ... Mmmmm ...

Here we are ! Your time has come, Marco. It is time for you to address this word. You've always said yes with your head, but let's face it: you've never understood shit.

We're cheerful, spontaneous and impertinent, like children who meet each other in kindergarten for the first time, right? I ask, she smiles and answers.

So, I don't want to know about scientific terms, let's simplify. The man has the sperm and the woman has the eggs. When the sperm fertilizes an egg, the woman becomes pregnant.

So far, so good.

She continues: While men produce sperm as if there was no tomorrow, with no expiration date, the woman, on the other hand, is already born with all the eggs she will need for a lifetime !!!

First thing I didn't know. A nice deposit in the ovaries of one or two million.

At the age of 20, she will generally still have 200,000, and then the number drops until reaching a cash fund of 2,000 around the age of 40.

Every month, during the fantastic period where she becomes particularly radioactive, the woman consumes a certain number of eggs from this deposit; then on average one matures, ready and waiting to be fertilized.

I'll simplify. It's as if the woman had been given a bag of colored balls as soon as she was born, and they had told her: "please, make them last for life". She rummages through the balls every month for the one with a particular color.

She rummages, rummages, rummages in search of the right one, and meanwhile some balls come out of the bag and end up getting lost. The woman was wasteful, you know, but in those days it was better not to let her know.

In assisted fertilization the gynecologist sucks in some of the balls that the woman is about to lose, while looking for the one of her favorite color!

Meanwhile, the man ??? Go watch some porn!

I see a scientist calling a doctor calling a lawyer calling a book editor who looks at me severely ... 'speaking words of wisdom, let it be'.

After having sucked them, he gives them to a biologist, who puts them in contact with the product created by the porno, fertilizing them in vitro.

With a syringe, the fertilized eggs are injected into the uterus, hoping that they will become an embryo. Unique and unrepeatable. Human Dignity.

Meryl had two human dignities, one male and one female, but let's talk about the two modes of assisted fertilization that our protagonist experienced, before reaching this wonderful goal.

Don't worry, we're finished with the scientific part for now.

REALLY COOL ITALIAN version...

Then the ATHENS version ...

REALLY COOL ITALIAN version:

Experimental tests in mega clinic with a private room.
All inclusive satellite TV. Nurses very well prepared, very polite,
well educated, everything in order, beautiful green green smocks.
You can also choose the color of the puree.

She goes down this hall with all marble and chandeliers.
Operating room. She is sleeping. Then she wakes up, goes out.
Waits. Goes home.

After two weeks they tell her it didn't go well. 6000 euros total,
1400 euros just for the room.

ATHENS version:

Hospital with state-of-the-art technology managed by doctors in
the 60s Italian style with cigarettes in mouths and holding cups of
coffee in giant personal cups.

The day of implantation they call it, they are ready to fertilize her.
Two hours of standard delay in the waiting room, where she waits
with all the others ... Italians. Green smocks but not the cool
green of Rome. Noisy, creaky gurney. They put her in a storage
closet the size of a gurney, a cherry, and a fat doctor. After
another hour delay, they draw back the curtain. Here comes the
doctor whose hand is the size of a basketball player's foot.
Naturally, without gloves, he pulls Meryl's legs up. Inserts the
syringe. Pat on the ass! "Good Luck". And he's gone! Pale
husband! Entire duration: 30 seconds.

Twins were born!

From that moment on she stops feeling Inadequate!

"It was the year of the first riots in Athens, and we were on the
opposite side of the clinic in the midst of the black blocs. I was

loaded with hormones, I didn't give a damn, I had to eat. I lept over some dumpsters! "

Closed airports, disorder, general chaos."They kept us for 3 days in the hospital, for free, and made us eat like wild boars. If we had left immediately, it probably wouldn't have gone as well as it did.

"In addition to the famous 30 seconds we stayed a week in Athens. 16 eggs were collected and fertilized. 8 survived, of which 4 were healthy. They implanted 3. 2 took root in the uterus.

Re-read for a moment. Yes, I said 4 were healthy!

In Italy, if the analysis had been done on in vitro fertilized eggs, on embryos, on human dignity, and discovered that they were unhealthy, they would have been implanted anyway. Not in Greece.
Italian law did not allow analysis on the embryo, but allowed the killing of a five-month fetus.

Treacher Collins Syndrome, or Franceschetti syndrome, or mandibular-facial dysostosis, have a hereditary pathology, and this pathology results from the analysis of fertilized eggs.

A year earlier, a state clinic proposed "let's try" with risk! Without any preventive psychological support! The "let's try" results were the third month that the child had the disease. Support was only offered later, after the decision was made to terminate the pregnancy in the fifth month. "Murder!" I don't use this word. Momma is using it!

In the fifth month it was found that her daughter's pathology was at a higher level than hers.

Using easy words he would have had greater aesthetic problems than she had. Bigger problems with society!No physical malformation below the neck. None!
No mental illness above the neck. None!

Meryl is against therapeutic abortion. Meryl accepted therapeutic abortion. "The pre-implantation examination allows you to ascertain whether the embryo, with less than a week of life, is healthy or not. If this examination were allowed, therapeutic abortion could be avoided. I'll carry my guilt with me for life. I'd rather have it than not having forced the birth of a daughter who throws herself off a bridge at 12 "

Meryl now has a hearing aid implant, no weird headband over her head that prevents her from going to the pool, playing volleyball. However, she continues to avoid games where the ball is present, and seldom goes to the pool. But today there is a place ...A place in the middle of your hair where you can rest the temples of your sunglasses!

I've been talking to her for a while, and I've forgotten her gaze seemed a bit sad. Now that I've seen her really sad!

Meryl always understood which side of the sidewalk to walk.
She instinctively knows where to put herself when she enters a club. She always wanted to be in control. No hangover. No drugs.

"Even though I try to pretend nothing has happened to my body, every February 11th I feel sick, that day I have symptoms"

Her birthday was the same day as mine, February 11th ... the day of Our Lady of Lourdes ... Born 34 years after my birth. She died the same day after 18 hours of labor. She wanted to see it ... Her name is Maria !

At the moment of death, if a priest is missing, anyone with the proper intention of giving baptism can, and in some cases must. It's even possible to baptize during pregnancy, if conditions are desperate. But she remembers that a priest did all this, and it was strange. It was as if he knew he was doing the right thing in the wrong ways.

I watch her. Her gaze is proud. In my eyes they're no longer sad.

We smile at each other. It's time to open the door, get out of the wonderful corner where we chatted, isolated from the world. The house is very sunny. Someone asks us ... "coffee ?"

Now that we understand what assisted fertilization is ... I got a taste for it, and I'm talking about the atom and the quantum; then we'll move on to the cheetah ecosystem and understand how to stop the ozone hole simply by eating carrots ...

I see a scientist calling a doctor calling a lawyer calling an book editor who looks at me severely ... 'speaking words of wisdom, let it be'!

- Track 3 -

Freedom of expression.

I am free to express myself as I believe.

If you're offended, if it hurts you, it's your problem!

I've heard these words many times, often out of my own mouth!

I was in Turkey sitting with Turgay, a friend of mine, who speaks Italian very well. There had been cartoons in Denmark about Mohammed that were stirring up controversy in the Islamic world.

In front of a glass of Turkish tea, with a cigarette in my hand, I was heating up, in fact, let's face it, I was getting angry with Turgay. The conversation had more or less these tones. "Holy shit, you come to us and we build mosques as well, and for a fucking cartoon you threaten us with death? Will this ever be anything but a backward culture! "Turgay doesn't get upset, he drinks tea and smokes a cigarette like me. He takes his German car keys, his wallet, and puts them in front of me!

"Marco, I think like you! I do the same job, I have a nice car, I earn well, and I've gained a lot of culture while traveling. You're right to be angry! I am too!

But...
IMAGINE.

If you were born poor, with no possibility of forming a balanced opinion on what is happening around you from television, newspapers or the internet. You have nothing, life has given you nothing, and will probably never give you anything.

You only have 2 things:
Your mother, and God.

IMAGINE.

If someone viciously insulted your mother, Marco, what would you do? "

I, Marco Perino,
I imagined.
I answered ...

"Probably ..."

and he goes on...

"If someone viciously insulted your God, Marco what would you do? I agree with you. But they have only this. We can choose. They can't! We can choose whether to offend and hurt. If we are truly evolved as we think we are. We will not do that !!! "

I reflect ...

It's difficult not to judge what's happening.

But I see shadows where everything was perfectly clear before.

Freedom of expression.

I'm free to express myself as I believe.

If you're offended, if it hurts you ...

Maybe... it's my problem too!

THE TRUCK DRIVER

No, not early in the morning. If you wanted to break my balls, you really succeeded. Why do I have to find this stuff in front of the warehouse door at five to eight in the morning? Couldn't you have arrived at ten or eleven like all the normal ones who leave somewhere around eight, do a little on the way, and then arrive here around ten or eleven? I already knew what I needed to do, and now all my plans are screwed.

I would have arrived at five to eight. I'd have gone to the locker to get the scissors and the pen. I would have greeted my colleagues quickly. I would have cut and folded all the cardboard boxes that they emptied the night before to warm up, and then the remaining time I would have brought the missing yarn for the looms in reserve.

Knitwear factory. Around nine, nine–thirty I would start sorting the pieces of fabric, dividing them by diameter, wool or cotton and, customer. And, at the same time, I would open and close the warehouse door for the various suppliers, vans that collect fabric, and small trucks that bring me other boxes of thread.

But a truck already parked in front of the warehouse before the day begins?

As a kid I loved adjustable models, the ones where the truck cab could be detached from a really long mega–trailer.
They had given me one only once. The mega–long trailer had double tires, three on each side; I took it from the box and had tried all six wheels on one finger. Yes, they would turn nicely on the linoleum floor.

Then there was the truck in front to be removed immediately!...
and it became another thing.
It had a red and blue cab with a flat black stripe behind it with a
hitch... And it was no useless. If I tried to launch it at full speed
against the wall, it would flip first. But if I attached the mega-
trailer to it, then ... No, I still couldn't launch it at full speed
against the wall, because it was twisted and after two attempts I
realized that those other cars had been built for the wall that my
mother had told me "at least these make them last a bit".

It had been built, to fit all the toy cars into it, at least, that was
the purpose I had assigned it. I opened the doors behind, I turned
around to see better, and one, two, three, four, six, seve ...
mmmmm, come on, if I push a little more ... crack ... okay, six
cars , and a door fell on the floor. And then yes, with two fingers I
pushed a full truck around the house, with the cars inside and life
made sense.

But at five to eight in the morning, a real truck doesn't make any
sense in the life of a warehouse worker. I go to the locker to get
the scissors and the pen. I pass a colleague who understands
from my face that it's better to pretend not to have seen me, and
I open the warehouse door. As soon as the factory is completely
opened, the left door of the truck opens. A guy gets out, the
truck driver! ... and he's dressed like a truck driver. Short shorts,
the kind of gray T–shirt that only truckers wear, and shoes that
are part shoes, part cowboy boots, and part beach sandals. I don't
know where they buy them, but only truck drivers have them.
After seeing his hands, I don't want to smile at him. They're full
of papers. If your hands are full of papers, this truck is fuller than
a truck with eight toy cars inside, and it's full of 120 pound boxes
of yarn that I'll have to unload pallet by pallet. I don't know where
to put them! This pisses me off so much that some of the guys
avoid having coffee at the machine to avoid eye contact. I hate
everyone, but I especially hate him ... The truck driver!

But the truck driver isn't stupid and he understood.
He says a brief good morning, hands me the paperwork, and then
he takes the pallet truck and brings the first pallet of eight boxes.
I take the forklift, I move the boxes, he brings me the others, I
move the boxes, and then ...Then the forklift battery dies. If he'd
warned me yesterday that he was arriving with the truck, I would
have charged it.

I also take a pallet truck, and after an hour his toy is completely
empty. Meanwhile my warehouse is full of empty boxes to
breakdown, the machines are about to stop because they've run
out of yarn, and I haven't had coffee yet!

I sign the delivery notes, go to close the warehouse and the truck
driver says ... "I also have to upload" and in that instant a part of
me dies forever.

I knew that sooner or later someone would come to get all those
rolls of coarse–yellow–mangy fabric that had occupied half the
warehouse for weeks, but they had assured me that I'd be warned
first. They were to be sorted, divided by date, batch, type of yarn,
machine. There were a ton of them, heavy ones too. From 40 to
50 lbs. And the pallet trucks couldn't be used for these. For these
we used our arms. Someone comes to give me a hand, but since
Murphy's law was in play that day, when that someone arrives,
another of those vans or small trucks shows up to unload and
load a couple stupid things. Two stupid things that, however, still
had to be searched, checked, and in the meantime ... The truck
driver and I load his truck by ourselves. And loading a truck,
inside the body of a truck, in the middle of summer ... It makes
you sweat! We're quickly transformed into two sweating pigs: one
disgusting warehouse worker and one disgusting truck driver. We
stink so bad that we start laughing, and with laughter we start

chatting. We finish loading, then he checks his notes written in pen on the flap of the box.

I check my hieroglyphs written with my pen. Do his and my accounts add up? No ! "Look, I'm never wrong" ... "I'm never wrong either" ... "Are you sure you counted the smaller one which was 16 instead of 20 and... yes? " "Let's check it all over again! "

We have a cluster–fuck that I wouldn't wish on anyone.

He comes back the next month, then the next, and our stinking together becomes a continual appointment. And while we are loading we talk about a billion things, and the words flow like gulps of beer at Oktoberfest. And then we laugh, I for his Modena accent, he for my 'boia faus. (Piemontese cursing) Those who pass in front of the loading dock ask themselves: "What do they have to laugh about, while working their asses off?"

He tells me about this meter which is used by the police to check how many hours he drives and how many hours he takes off. If he drives more than he should, he risks a fine. So, he's only a two hour drive from home, but he still has to stop at the motorway restaurant to sleep. Shower, and then bunk for thirteen hours, before he can get back on the road. Once home, he argues with his wife, with whom he has been married for ten years, and ends up sleeping on the sofa, without her.

Then one day he didn't arrive, either in front of my warehouse or at his wife's house.

"I'm finished for good!"

The marriage is peaceful; he doesn't care about the interests of his wife who lives for stores and shopping. He's a quiet type, without too much nonsense in his head. He believes in human relationships and tries make as little trouble as possible in this world.

He comes from a family where expressing feelings delicately is not a habit, and he's used to it. In company it's what his 'character' does, an idiot who entertains. He's a person who knows who he is..

Then, as time goes by, age begins to smooth out new life needs in him. There is nothing wrong with shopping and stores, but at a certain point he just can't live like that anymore. And with the wife, the family, he can't express what he feels, can't do it too loud, then might people criticize. He tries. But after a while hardly at all. "I don't give a damn about what people say ..."

In company he's no longer fun. When a discussion has neither head nor tail, he says what he thinks. This alienates everyone. Don't like him anymore. They walk away, they say that the funny guy has started putting them off.

And he has four friends left. The most uncool ones. The only real ones.

He doesn't understand how to express what's inside.
He knows neither how it is done nor how it is expressed.
And he can't even explain to his friends what he feels he has to do because he doesn't know either. A colleague of his continues to talk to him about energy, about a world of energy. He is curious, yes, but he doesn't understand anything.

One day in his truck on the highway he sees an advertising sign: "Introductory courses to Shiatsu". He doesn't know at all what this thing is, but he really likes the word. It's a word that has entered him.

And now all of you make a mental effort with me ...
Imagine Vasco Rossi's accent saying:

"Sciàttsuuu ... What a beautiful word ... Who knows what the fuck
it means".

... when you've stopped laughing, we'll move on ...

He wrote down that phone number. After two weeks he was
enrolled in the course and his new life began. I never saw him
again at five to eight.

He's 33 years old. He discovers that each of us has an inner
strength that we don't use because of societal preconceptions.
Rules and nonsense that don't allow you to live what we were
born for. Each of us is born an artist, and an artist is not just
someone who becomes famous. Even the accountant, the
carpenter, the kindergarten teacher can be, if they're bringing out
the most from the depths of their being. And he understands that
he could have been another kind of man. An artist.

He understands energy, he begins to practice. And with practice,
there are obstacles. And with obstacles he begins his journey to
become great.

As a black belt, his whole life begins again starting from the white
one; he goes back to his very first job, one of those jobs you can't
wait to change, but which now, with new self-awareness, he'd
never change. This job gives him time, and he needs time.

He continues his course with acupressure, Shiatsu. Because
shiatsu is not a massage, but his lifestyle. He does shiatsu while
filling the fridge, and while choosing what to put in the fridge. He
does shiatsu while chewing and also while listening to her chew.

At the same time he carries on what was a primitive hobby, and was more from memory than history: photography.

At first he studies technique, but then develops its energy. If he photographs a Vietnamese, he's not interested in the wrinkled face, everyone's seen that. He's interested in the soul. Not everyone has seen that. He sees the soul in the movements of people.

Maybe ... That's what he was born for ... Here's the way to go ... Combine Shiatsu with photography. Move energy with one and tell it with the other.

But it's not easy. Sometimes it's enormously difficult ...

and then he looks at the sky ...
And with his Vasco Rossi accent ...

"Oh, you, superior strength or whatever you're called, could you give me a hand huh ... Holy shit!"

And it works...

He's always given what he needs ... No more, no less.

Now he lives with a new partner he met by chance ...
But it's not easy. They are simultaneously very different, and very "identical". They fight in separate rooms, but it's the same; they sleep every night in two different rooms. He snores too much.

The arguments on the sofa no longer happen. If there's anger, they share, talk, dissect the problem. They do not look for the wrongs and the reasons, but look for ways to resolve situations. And it works.

They travel when they can, but monuments are the least of their interests.

They're interested in seeing where people throw their trash, how they move on the street, where they go to work, how they live every day.

And so what do you want me to dream about?
Billboards, TV broadcasts, books ...

No !

He dreams of living a good life, without being invasive to others and to the world.

He dreams of retiring and being able to devote himself to his passions.

Energy and photography.

In the mean time he's become a highly regarded shiatsu teacher, but he continues to remain a very quiet person who believes in human relationships.

They have a small spectacular vegetable garden where they grow spring onions ... Those with the accent of Vasco Rossi ...
And when they have two cents, they go around the world.
When they don't have money they stay at home.

He's a truck driver who dreams of living a good life.
One who doesn't have too much nonsense in his head.
One who lives his quiet, simple life ...

... His life as an artist!

But I'm not fooled. In my opinion he's lying.

He just wants to ...
... I turn around to get a better look, and one, two, three, four,
six, sev ... mmmmm, come on, that if I push a little more ...
crack ... okay, six cars, and a door remained in the floor.
And then yes, with two fingers he pushes the load too ... And
once the traffic jam is overcome, movement returns ...

... His life, yours, has a completely different meaning.

But be careful ...

In the end one always has to carry a little load!

Asimov, I came here to buy two or three Asimov's books.

It's four in the morning. Four in the morning is the worst when one can't sleep. At three o'clock one still has hope, but at four, even if he succeeds, what sleep, three hours? I've never suffered from insomnia, but tonight, or this morning, I'm agitated. It takes a lot of willpower to get out of bed at four in the morning and give up sleep.

I don't have breakfast, it's not breakfast time. I dress in the stuff that's on the chair, I don't look in the mirror. I start the car. I drive on the deserted street and park near the boulevard, the only pedestrian street we have in the city.

There is just me and a little mouse, who as soon as he sees me is dumbfounded for a few seconds as if asking: what's this guy doing on a shopping street at four in the morning? Yeah! What am I doing here?

In a few hours I have my first book presentation.
I have never submitted a book. I've never even seen a book presentation. How you do it? What needs to be said?
Will it be the way I want it to be? What if I make a fool of myself? And then they realize I'm not really a writer?

I stop in front of the window where I had bought two or three Asimov's books.

They had put them in a small package for me; I take a side street a few hundred feet to an entrance. I ask for confirmation on the visiting hours and they give me assistance.

He's surprised to see me, we haven't seen each other for a while. But we're friends and I give him the books, he's truly happy. He loves Asimov and he loves all science fiction. When he talks to me about Alien he can't help but emphasize the A ... It's a word you just can't say in a low voice. Then he tells me about the others. Those who are his friends, the ones he frequents and whom I don't even know well. He hasn't seen them since. They were always there to slap him on the back, to make him feel superior, to ask him for advice, to get help when they ended up in the shit a little below the ankle. And he's strong. He helped them. A little bit to remain the strongest one in the eyes of all, and a little bit for that cursed heart of gold.

He hasn't seen them since.

I have to go to work. My shift is from two to ten.
Thanks for the books; imagine, you would have done it too.

A year, damn, I don't know how he did it. It was four in the morning and I was returning home desperate. She had left me and I didn't know where to turn.

I pass his house. He's in the middle of the street with his arms wide open. What's he doing at four in the morning in the middle of the street??? I have to brake. I have to stop. He points to his house, and insists that I enter. I'm crying. How could he tell?

I still wonder today.

He makes me sit down, he makes me talk, he makes me vent. Then he makes me go home to sleep. He made me calm down.

And now that I'm in front of this bookshop where I bought Asimov? There are a lot of white books in the window with my name on them. I'm scared.

I think of him, I think of that night and I think of that morning.

I get the car and go home to sleep. Although I slept only a few hours I slept very well.

He made me calm down.

How strange to be here in front, to be here in front alone,
lying on these flat and gray bricks in front of the entrance.
Looking at it with my head resting in my hands.

How many times have I been here. Always so many people here.

Impossible to be alone right now.

Especially now.

Children, elderly people, adults, wheelchairs, cars, ambulances,
lighter sellers, grandparents, parents, children. My grandparents;
my parents; I; the ambulance. Two guards pointing directions and
to the right, then straight down the hall. A slightly uphill ramp
and then the stairs. The elevator was on the left, but it was slow,
so slow. As it went down I saw the numbers of the floors light up
and remain fixed for too long. There was no floor where it didn't
stop. Doors that open and doors that close. Embarrassed looks in
forced company ...Then again, slowly, to the next floor.

My patience has a maximum range of two, so took the stairs, just
to the left.

It's so big that you can see it from the freeway. This discolored
yellow brick, a bit higher and to the right of the city. How strange
it is, seen from so close. Lying with his head in his hands, alone!

The new one has now been inaugurated. The noise is now a few
miles away. Here silence has remained, so silent that it allows you
to listen to the wind.

The wind in front of the old hospital in Biella.

We're on lunch break, and I left the group a few minutes earlier. I wanted this moment all to myself. After so many hours in the midst of people, I always need to isolate myself a little.

Then I wanted to listen to this hospital.

The first days we worked here, I observed it. Enter and go to the right, where years before I had entered with the sirens screaming, and hear no other noises than those of people setting up lights or cameras; not the normal ones of an emergency room.

I saw a room that used to be for doctors and nurses, the same doctors and nurses who made me lie down, just after the ambulance blue sirens.

In that room their signatures, their thoughts, their melancholy. It's not easy to abandon the old for the new, especially if the old is filled with memories, years and blood; of life and death.

Those who work with me these days are not local. They work in a faded yellow building on the side of a town near the mountains. A place like in every city.

But this place gives me goosebumps.
This is where they put my arm and foot in a cast.
This is where I screamed as I clung to a curtain with back pain.
This is where I slept in the midst of those who complained, while my mother tried to rest her head at the foot of my bed.

I had to listen to this hospital a bit.
I had to be alone with him for a while.
Stay close to him.
Stay close to my memories.

I manage to be alone, with my head in my hands for half an hour, then I see him approaching. We haven't seen each other in a long time.

He approaches slowly. I know he won't do his job; not with me.

I sit up. He sits next to me. We smile a little. We're two old friends who reunite after many years.

But at a funeral.

We are two spades from the same deck.
Neither hearts nor clubs nor diamonds at the start.
No gift.
Not for us.

When two bad seeds are born with the same deck, not many words or smiles are needed.

If there had been someone else alone in my place, doing the same job as me, he would have played; he would push the prey towards the trap. He would take home information, news, maybe some gossip. But not with me.

He sits with me. Looks at the yellow block. Listens to the wind. He nods his head.

With us the law of nature works.
That law that animals still respect, perhaps by instinct, perhaps by intelligence.
And in man ...
And in man doesn't work.

The nature of two spades from the same deck, of two wolves from the same pack.

No heart, no flower, and not even any painting can change our nature. It's not bought. It's not sold.

I'm working on someone else's dream. A dream that I don't care a bit about. A dream that I've never dreamed of and therefore for me it's not a dream. There are those who dream of music; there are those who dream of books; there are those who dream of films; there are those who dream of houses; there are those who dream of love; there are those who dream. And if you play music for those who dream of love, they will listen, but they will dream of love. And if you give love to those who dream of movies, they will love but they will dream of movies.

Around me I see enthusiasm, smiles, commitment, plans, for a great dream. But because of someone else's great dream, which allows me to work and pay my rent, I am neglecting mine.
Every dream is jealous, and I am jealous of my dream, and even if theirs is brilliant; I don't care.

It took me years to understand my dream. But he had already understood it then, when they put us in the same deck.
When they put us in the same deck ...

We were twelve.

A little man who spoke with bad audio. One of those movies where you always have to stand with the remote control in hand to increase or decrease the volume. He whispers and then suddenly without warning ... AAAAHHHH ... a scream of enthusiasm. Back to normal and then a scream again ... OH MY GOD ... this time he's desperate. What the hell is he doing? How is it possible they let him do it? He borders on ridiculous, indeed, he wants to be ridiculous ... Just keep listening to him, and watching him. He does not stand still. I can't focus on him. He moves too much.

I don't understand what you mean, what you're doing. He makes me laugh a little. I look around and he makes others laugh too. The literature teacher laughs too. Then he stops ... ... and then silence ...

And then we understand.

We are twelve to fourteen years old. That little man is a priest, a desperate teacher of religion. Desperate if he can't find the words to describe what his soul is telling him.

He showed our deck Nazis and prophets, Martin Luther King and imaginary double bass players. He made us sing and dance gospel. To collect cotton from slaves and blacks. Build pyramids. Made us imprison and free us from Jews. We watched Nebuchadnezzar having the dreams of the prophet Daniel read. We watched a wolf from our pack water the plant of life with imaginary water.

And he, yes, the silent one sitting next to me now, he was the demiurge who shouted and launched the big bang: "The explosion composed of fine, luminous dust".

That little man there, forcing you with the remote control in hand. He made us all act; all of us ! He made us all laugh; all of us ! And, he changed everything for both of us!

Neither hearts nor flowers nor diamonds at the start. No gift. Not for us who have decided to try, like that little man, to listen to the soul. He could tell us though ... It felt bad!

I discovered it late, but my partner in spades, at fifteen, already knew what his dream was. He was convinced that he already understood everything ...

And he was right!

High schools, different places and schools.
We both struggle, yet they say we are smart.
What will this intelligence ever be?
Why are we struggling?

At the end of the year we both have to make up time.
I commit myself and without knowing what I dream of, I pass to
the second year. He's committed and knowing what he dreams,
he fails in tears. He escapes through the backdoor of the school.

They were the tears of a child falling down the stairs while
everyone is watching him. If they hadn't looked at him, he
wouldn't have cried. If they hadn't looked, he might not even
fallen. He would keep running towards his dream.

But the shame. The shame of those who were watching, and who
did not want to know about dreams. A piece of paper. Immediate
work. Safe work.

He had already understood that to do what he wanted to do it was
not only necessary to commit; Support was needed. Support.
Without it made no sense.

The journalist.

A vocation.

He would have made those who read it scream AHHH and
OHMYGOD. He would interview and listen. Uncomfortable
thoughts and doubts. Set traps in forbidden territories.

No piece of paper was suitable for fifteen years. The parents
wanted a job for him right away. But he already knew. We already

knew for him. Like when mimicked famous broadcasters on bus trips, standing next to the driver. When he introduced and entertained us more than any radio. While interviewing and commenting.

We already knew that. We of his deck.

Today the crisis is a blessing. No work right away.
If anyone has a vocation ...Give it a shot ! There's nothing more to lose.

But when there's certainty, the soul cannot listen to it.
You must not to listen to the soul, otherwise you make people laugh. You're not in a movie or on television. You can't. What do you think you can dream of? Don't you want to be one of those interviewers? Or be interviewed? Come on, don't laugh.
Don't you want to become like that little man there?

You're not a heart, a flower or a painting.

You're a spade. The spade has to be grounded ...

"Where is it written?"
... don't contradict!

We're from the same pack.

Very different, but nature works for us.

We agree.

Crisis is a blessing for dreams.

I lost sight of the little man. Instead, he continues to frequent him for many years. He begins working in the theater and opera. The cinema. On reflections full of sensitivity and rhetoric. On fantastic, spiritual discoveries.

Yet, despite the injustices, the parents, the money, the wrong women, he still loves to stop in front of a painting, a flower or a heart; a panorama. If you get lost in the eyes of a person imagining their life, it is thanks to that little man there.

No gift.

Not to us ...

... But that little man there.

A journalist and perhaps a writer or perhaps a musician.

We should be talking about a big dream, but we set up the lights and cameras ourselves. We're smiling a little. We're two old friends who meet again after many years, but at a funeral.

We look at the faded yellow block together.

We listen to the wind.

He won't do his job.
Not with me.

The law of nature works for us.

He walks away slowly ...

He could tell though ... It hurt!

- Track 6 -

Stop and trust. If only he had done so by now she would be in the sky.

She had entered through an open window. It was spring and time to finally change the air in the house. She flew very frightened close to the ceiling. The window was just a few feet down, but she was too scared to go out. I watched her. I tried to climb a ladder to get her. I tried to direct her lower with a broom. Nothing. She was too scared. It flew fast from one corner of the room to the other. It flapped its wings with agonizing speed. A swallow. If only she'd let herself be taken. If only she stopped. If only she had trusted. I would have taken her, I would have given her a gentle caress on the head, and I would have put her at the window; free to fly to its sky.

I leave the windows open. I go out. I forget about it.

A few days go by and a strange smell comes from behind a piece of furniture. I move it. It was her. It was what remained of her.

If only she'd let herself be taken. If only she had been still.
If only she had trusted.

Today it's my turn.
Wait.
Trust in waiting.
Yet.

I did everything I had to do.
I did everything I could do.
I studied, sowed, proposed, worked, dreamed.
I followed all the signs.
I did it with commitment, perseverance, determination, tenacity.

I've done all this but, I don't see anything moving.
What if I got it all wrong?
What if I misunderstood?

Wait.
Trust in waiting.
Again.
Have faith ...
Again.

I'm scared...
... Again.
But today I'm still. Perspective. I don't control anything.
I trust you.

Put me at the window you prepared for me.
I flew a lot and I flapped my wings a lot.
I'm tired.

As you place me at the window.
I'm going to have a beer!

A GLASS OF WATER

Try to fill half a glass of water. Take the classic glass of Nutella, and once it's half filled, observe it.

Observe it.

What's a half glass of water good for? To wet that little cactus we have in the windowsill? To drink? I hardly seems that I've drunk anything with half a glass of water. Ah, yes, that's the dose you need to make that recipe that ...Add half a glass of water to prevent sticking.

No ! We're wrong: "you can make a mistake in life"

Here, if you add half a glass of water, you pay for it.
You're plugged to the machine for another quarter of an hour.

And how would you live if you were forced to plug in to a machine for an extra half hour for a glass of water?

Now she's talking to me while playing on the computer, he tells me that ...

She no longer sleeps at night. She hasn't slept at night since her mother passed away.

She told everyone she wanted to go to Lourdes before she died. So why did someone give her that trip? Couldn't they understand it? Couldn't they give her something else? Did they have to give her a trip to Lourdes? She returns from the pilgrimage, and not a week goes by that ...she's no longer herself.

The doctor made it clear, it's nothing, she's just in shock.
It's all psychosomatic. Rest, tranquilizers, mineral salts.

Shock, psychosomatic.

Words.

Words of bullshit.

Okay, let's take tranquilizers and mineral salts, but she still doesn't sleep at night.. These aren't words, these are facts.

She tries to sleep in the kitchen. Puts a pillow on the table to try to sleep. In the morning, when her husband comes home from the night shift, he finds her. Bent over the table, awake.

Her body begins to break down. Her feet swell. She's out of breath.

Psychosomatic. Shock.

Tranquilizers and mineral salts.

Every time she goes down the stairs, twenty steps, she has to stand still for ten minutes. She waits in the car ten minutes to catch her breath.

The doctor was definite, it's nothing, yet she really struggles to breathe. She feels her heart is tired. She's really tired. She's too tired.

And her heart is only 38 years old. She's only 38 but she already has two grown children, has been married for more years than she lived without a husband, and feels damn tired.

Coming home from the night shift, he finds her bent over the table. Again ?

That's enough!

Emergency ward.

She can't stand lying in bed. The doctor notices that something is wrong. Thorough blood and urine tests and the verdict comes:

"She has severe kidney failure with a creatinine level already at eight!"

" And what does that mean... Is it serious? "

The next morning she is "pinched" to check how much water she has in her body. The creatinine is at eleven.

"But what is this creatinine? Is it serious? "

"No, she's young, we'll give her an AV fistula. Then she'll go on dialysis! "

Dialysis? That thing that Lucio Battisti also did? That thing where they put tubes in you and make your blood run 'til it's clean? Then after a few days gets dirty and they have to clean it again?

Forever?

She starts to cry.

The doctor looks at her indifferently: "When you're done tell me, then I'll explain the rest".

She continues to cry.

"She's young and has the option of a transplant, but first ..."

First...

An entire month's hospitalization, only for exams, just to assess the situation.

At home the husband is destroyed. He doesn't want to eat. He no longer wants to do anything. He won't accept what his daughter cooks.

She goes home and for three months they feed her inedible products: protein-free treatments. Every two weeks, tests to see if the creatinine was stabilizing or rising. Creatinine: waste chemical produced by our body, by our muscle metabolism. But who knows

this stuff? In a healthy woman, the value fluctuates between 0.5
and 1.1 milligrams per deciliter. Its value ranged between 11 and
14. If the kidneys are not working, the fluids are not disposed of,
and creatinine rises.

Dialysis begins.
The first person she sees is a foreign woman, apparently the most
negative person in the world. She's sitting in the waiting room.
She's eating a packet of crackers. "Are you new, the first time? Ah
you'll see what awaits you! "

They will become very good friends.

After the comfortable welcome, she enters a room for beginners
by herself. The novices. There's only her, the head physician and
a nurse. She sees a bed, a booth, a cart with medicines, an
armchair with a bedside table; a machine, a monitor with tubes.
They take her blood pressure. They tell her to relax, and poke her
with match-sized needles!

The nurse sits in a chair. She doesn't leave her alone. Never.
Watches her reactions. Monitors her heartbeats.

Dialysis begins. The tubes are one for blood and one for water.
You only see the blood, the water is filtered. The water must be
filtered from the blood in 4 hours.

The nurse tries to get her to talk about this and that, but she only
thinks negative things. She remembers nothing else this first
time, only the negative.

But she remembers when she got home. She wanted to go back to
the doctor, as the patient with the imaginary illness, using
mineral salts: "You can make a mistake in life ..." these are the
words! Mineral salts are rich in potassium.

Potassium further damaged the kidneys.

She didn't report it. She didn't feel it was worth it. Maybe "you can
make a mistake in life ..."

Maybe "you can make a mistake in life ..." but in reality, you can't very often.

But at that point she had other things to fight for.

She was destroyed. Dead tired. Without strength.

Depression.

The family bonds together. The husband offers to donate a kidney, but the blood type is different. The son offers himself, but he can't, a child cannot donate to the parent. Her father offers, but is already receiving cancer treatment.

"She's young and has the possibility of a transplant, but first ..."

First...

Twelve years. Three times a week. Four hours a day.

Twelve years in which everything changes. Changes the way you eat, and especially drink. And you're always thirsty. And you can't drink that much. So you eat, you suck on ice to get the feeling of drinking.

Between one day of dialysis and the next you couldn't gain six pounds. **An extra glass of water in two days?** Half an hour more of dialysis. The one after Christmas and New Year, of course, but also the one after each weekend, the only times where two days passed instead of one between one sitting and the next.

"I've never been to jail but it's like ...
Only Christmas and New Year.
All other days don't count.
To move one day you have to ask for permission.
If you don't show up, the police will be sent to you for endangering your life ... "

... they send the police!

Holidays?
Where?
How?
You have to book a hospital wherever you go.
But wherever you want to go ...

The arms...
The looks...

In the supermarket, observed as if she were a drug addict.
She ignores it but every now and then has to justify:
"I'm not a junkie. I'm on dialysis."

"She is young and has the option of a transplant, but first ..."

First...

Eight operations, some right and some wrong.
Everything is regulated.
Her. The family.
Try not to weigh her down.
Try not to disturb even the nurses, the doctors.
Try not to argue with people she's forced to see every two days,
three times a week, always...Unless a transplant ...

Yeah, a transplant.

Four hours is a long time to spend in a lounge chair.
Thoughts.
Solitude.
Why?

Why do they all pass by?

A group is formed in some way; somehow you become friends.
A seven-bed room becomes company. It's hard to go there, it's
always hard to go there, but somehow you laugh, and you pass
the time. We know each other. We talk. Joke. One gets you coffee

today and the next day it's my turn; and then a bed remains
empty:
Transplant!
She's happy. Six remain.
Then two empty beds:
another transplant.
She's happy.
Then five empty beds:
transplant!
She's...
Then it's only she and him. He's only been here three months,
she's been in the chair for years. A few days later she doesn't see
him. "Where is he? " "They called him. Transplant "

And she can't!
She's not happy.
She's alone.
She arrived first. Why is she the only one left?
She starts to cry. It's not fair, 12 years, he had three months.
There is no consolation.

She was never even called as second, as they say here, at least
you're next if the first called had problems. Some of her friends
have been called several times. One even fourteen times as
second, before having the transplant. Her never. Never first, never
second, never anything.

And the machine turns ...
It does what it has to do in its four hours.
That machine keeps her alive.
That machine is her life saver.
She lives because of that machine.

In twelve years she's met hundreds of people with this problem ..
Many die, more than 50%. Most from heart attacks, strokes, not
because of the machine. But after a while you no longer feel like
living with the machine. In twelve years governments change, the
geographies of certain states change, history changes and also
many laws; however, the husband does not change. In all this he
has always been present. If he could, he would have attached
himself to the machine.

Tired all this time, yes, very tired. Nervous. Twelve years
His woman didn't even have desires anymore. She lives because
of the machine.

They begin psychological therapy. Whole days of chatting because
now after twelve years she can't take it anymore. She falls into
depression. She can no longer stand the machine, dialysis, tubes,
water, ice.

She wants to drink a fucking glass of water without being forced
to spend an extra half hour on the machine.

My phone rings.
It is the middle of the night.
It's my father.
... my father never calls me!

"I'm about to take your mother to the hospital ...
tomorrow morning they'll do the transplant! "

I put the phone down.
I sit on the sofa.
I look at the void.
I'm empty.
I don't cry, I don't laugh.
Twelve years.
Not even a lifetime of meditating could lead me to such a
completely empty head.

But half an hour earlier.

"When they called it was one in the morning. I didn't want to
answer the phone. I didn't have to go on dialysis the next day.
Over the years, every time it rang, I hoped it was a hospital.
This time there was nothing, the idea didn't even enter the
antechamber of my brain. I thought they were kidding me. I'm not
going there. Shock, this was shock "

"But at one-thirty in the morning does it seem I'm calling you as joke?

Do you want to go? "

"No. I'm not moving. I won't leave my house "

"Go! "

And...

And now that she can, she's no longer thirsty.

Now, more than drinking, she wants to eat big salads.
And cheese. Lots of cheese.

Perhaps she was a shepherdess, perhaps a farmer, the fact remains that before she loved pasta, carbonara, pizza, now it's cheese; lots of cheese. She doesn't give a damn about pasta and pizza!

She's talking to me while she's playing video games.
She looks tired. She won the game.

Now she and my father watch movies and TV programs at three in the morning. They no longer have schedules. They wake up late in the morning like someone returning from the disco.

He grumbles that she spends a lot of time playing video games, but then he lights a cigarette and has a laugh ...

After she unplugged the machine ...

... desires.

ACT THREE
They judged me

Your eyes saw my unformed body; all my days were
written in your book and ordained for me before one
of them came to be.

Psalm 139.16

- Track 15 -

I'm the football goalkeeper. The last man. If you lose it's my fault and if you win ...... ah, you know what I mean?

I play on one of those country teams that are destined for slaughter. They can't drop any further back, they're already last in the worse category.
And we play to win, we've never entered the field just to participate. But when we win it happens due to a concomitance of eclipses, comets, and Murphy's laws for the adversaries; and then the whole village goes crazy with joy.

I was joking ... Not even the people of the village come to watch our games anymore.

But we train every week. Mud, snow, mud that becomes ice, snow that becomes mud. We're there ...Runs, cones, schemes ... and finally the match.

Each of us gives up our surname and becomes the famous footballer of the moment. I was Pagliuca or Zenga against the best strikers in Rome, Juventus, Inter and Milan.

It's one of those medium games.

At this point we can only aim to make the lower half of the classification.

Even if we won them all, we would never finish first, but we want to avoid finishing last. For sure.

A short twelve-mile trip.

Dressing, shirt, shin guards and shoes.

I put on my gloves, moisten them like a ritual.
Like before every game I isolate myself.
Concentration. Whatever the stakes are.

...Concentration.

The referee arrives in the locker room. We take turns walking in front of him calling out our surname and jersey number ...
Perino ... One ...And then out ... Coin toss: "ball or field?" Field !

I go to my goal and start marking signs in the small area; those lines will help me understand where and how to exit when an opponent approaches. I'll need them to narrow access to the goal.

He must see me getting bigger and bigger as I get closer to him and move away from the posts. If he fakes me out, it's fucked ...

Kick-off whistle.

Half way through the first period and everything goes smoothly. The other team is also from the bottom of the classification. There are no particular vibrations on one side or the other. A few fouls, complaints, someone on sidelines calling someone else a bastard, all normal.

We remain goalless.

I suffer from soccer goalkeeper syndrome. If I make a good save at the beginning of the game, a ball will no longer enter even if you hit me in the face; I'll block it before I die. But if at first I make a goof, a wrong movement, an escaped ball, I'll be devastated for the rest of my days ...

until the next game.

I have the football goalkeeper syndrome even when I play music, if I screw up the first notes, I can only refund you the concert ticket.

In this particular first half I don't have any syndrome symptoms. My saves aren't bad. I deflected a ball with my fists to the corner. I comfortably caught a ball from my knees headed for goal, but with the panache and intensity of a turtle on his way to work. I'm stoked. I'm focused.

Then...

A Free kick outside the box for the opponents.
I have to position the 'wall.' I ask for four men.
The shot is pretty close so I want them to cover the near post well. I'll be on the second post ready to dive.

I scream ... To the right ... Stop ... Stay closed ... Come on!
I make them feel we're there, we're on the right track.
The referee stands on the other side of the area.
A swarm of people pushing there, but I'm on the second post ...

I won't screw up today ...

Nothing goes by me today!

The opponent takes a run. Shoots! He doesn't shoot towards the first post where I placed the wall ...Or towards the second where I control the entire goal ...No!

He completely misses the shot.

Shanks it. His shot is worse than mine when I was eight years old, a time when my technique dictated that I would never play outside the goal box.

I was made for the hands, not the feet.
The ball was still struck hard, very hard.
What did it strike?

The referee!

The referee who was on the opposite side of the world from any playable action. The referee who was where a referee was supposed to be during a free kick.

The referee is hit hard, and the only thing he can do to protect his manhood is turn his back. The ball bounces off his back ...
Around the wall ...

And enters the goal!

I'm motionless and open-mouthed.
All the other 21 players on the field are in awe.
Even the referee is speechless.
Then he blows the whistle ...
Indicates the center of the field ...

And confirms the goal.

Even today I've never heard anything more unfortunate in the history of a football goalie. It happened to me, it really happened to me. Whether the referee acted as a post, whether it was correct or not, at that moment, I didn't care anymore. It wasn't just the football goalkeeper syndrome; a shit storm had started.

As if one could judge good and evil. Right and wrong.

He takes a ball and overturns all logic. Which side should I be on? In the middle, right, left? Which side, if he gave me the goal?

If the referee makes a mistake and compromises the whole game,
how can I stay focused?

Ten goals we're scored against me. The opponents mocked me.
My teammates were embarrassed.
I was finished.
The referee screwed me!

I'm quitting football.

A few years later, my sister's boyfriend tries to convince me to
play again. This time it's an amateur championship ... "Come on,
just for fun".

I accept...And I really enjoy it. I put on my gloves, ritually moisten
them. I isolate myself every game like before. Concentration.
Whatever the stakes are ...
Concentration.

I'm carefree, the ranking position is no longer important.
I make a lot of goofs, but there are many more saves, even those
with penalty kicks.

They call me 'The Enforcer.'

After the championship we were in the top half of the
classification, a very respectable half. And by racking up attack
and defense numbers, we were the best defense in the league.
I was the one who conceded the fewest goals.
I'm happy...

... also because at the end of the last game ... with a big smile ... I
gave away my gloves.

I wouldn't put them on again!

I've always liked his father. One of those men who transmits peace. While he speaks, while he works, and also while he screams the twenty-four words that I prefer not to give to the censors. He's at peace with himself even when he gets mad!

Sometimes he sat telling simple things to us, like cutting wood or the lawn, that wine versus that cheese. It's never bored us, quite the contrary. His stories have always managed to lead us to questions or laugh, like when he found a woodworm in a plant. He took it in his hand, observed it attentively ...

And then he decided to eat it!

But why?

"To know what a woodworm tastes like!"

Simple isn't it?

Yet he is not simple.
He's a professor.
He protested in '68.
He got married, happily married ...
... And with his wife he decides not to have children.

His mother also protested in '68.
She's a ballsy woman, sure of herself ..
She's also not simple.
She's also a teacher.
She got married too, to a professor.
She too decides not to have children with her husband ...
But she gets pregnant; a daughter.

One day the father forgets his car keys an office;
retraces his steps, opens the door, says hi to his future wife
quickly because she's in a meeting, and she catches his glance.
With that glance she falls in love with him at first sight ... Love at
first sight. That glance doesn't believe in love at first sight ...
Yet ... That glance already has a daughter, and in the meantime
she's holding the train of a wedding dress.

That loving glance, in a self-confident woman, which is not
easy ...What happened in 1968 ...It will be his mother.

She changes everything to be transferred to where the man who
forgot the keys works. She succeeds. They start working together.

His father is happily married, but his mother is different.
They understand each other more, they laugh more.
Are you still happily married?

There were no photos to browse on a smartphone to look for a
double life. If there had been they wouldn't have downloaded that
application anyway. They don't want to become lovers.
Neither one wants this.

A woman born only for that man. Her father.
A man born only for that woman. His mother.

She leaves her husband and goes to live alone.

Months go by, years go by.
Then love breaks the levees.
True love always breaks the levees.
The word lovers is wrong. They are in love.

Almost four secretive years.

Maybe the wife simply didn't want to know.
Four years before they decide to live together.
Four years, before the thirty-two that they remained together.
Always in love!

They will remain two very independent people. They will work on
themselves a lot. Together they will reach such a level of
awareness that they will be willing to do anything, even to lose
each other. And together accept everything that society could not
accept.

Love.
True love.
Only love.

But years had to pass before the worm man obtained support.
The support of a very small country with an even smaller flock.
The solidarity of those who hadn't had the courage to make the
same choices.

For love...
The only true love.

Marriage is a very difficult job. Many crises; all survived.
The biggest one, bigger than all the others, a pregnancy loss.
The gynecologist warns her of possible problems for the fetus. A
crisis both as a couple and as individuals. They are that child. It's
horrible to face such a thing; for both of them! In the end they
decide together.

That child will not be.

Women who have abortions can become wonderful mothers;
she was!

Another son will arrive years later, the brother of who is telling me all this.

Their daughter ...

... She claims she didn't get much from her mother! During adolescence she also felt a deep hatred towards her. Towards this strong personality. But after a while she understands her strength. She accepts her guidance. Her opinion becomes more and more important, in each of her choices. Despite the clashes, she has always sought approval. Despite the clashes, she has always been free to make mistakes. Despite the clashes, she has always been free to choose her future independence.

And with the ease of her father when he chose to eat a woodworm, she arrived home one day, still a teenager, with a university textbook in hand: "I would like to become a obstetrician!" And the two parents who had protested in 1968 laughed and ask questions ...But why? "I read it in the manual ... It looks cool."

Simple isn't it?

Yes, all simple. Because their daughter is telling me everything ... She's a obstetrician today.

A obstetrician who had to learn to walk on her own legs without parental approval. At least not both of them.

Her mom was diagnosed with cancer. She got sick while she was planning her wedding. She managed to be there, but was sedated waiting to "cut the lights" the following year.

The obstetrician doesn't cry while she tells the story. Instead, she laughs a lot. Looking at her, she seems nothing like a obstetrician. She's funny and I can't help but laugh with her.

She tells me about her shifts in the hospital. Eight hours during the day or ten at night. And every day ...Every bloody day ...She finds herself on average with two new babies in hand. Sometimes one ... Sometimes three ...Three new babies in hand ...Sometimes six!

And we laugh!

And despite seeing births every bloody day, she tries to describe me the magic she feels ...That she feels every time ...Whenever they open their eyes for the first time!

The first breath ...

And then yes ... Sometimes she cries too ...
Especially if she sees fantastic parents around her.
Parents who love each other ... and that she often doesn't
recognize outside the hospital.

She tells me that women are no longer themselves during childbirth. They transform and change shape. They must be animals again. They have to let go of their mind and body to give birth.They find strength they didn't think they had. And then hear fathers say to their friends...

"I didn't think she was like this ...

So strong..."

What if they don't let themselves go ???

"If they're too cerebral ...

They give birth to shit! "
Simple huh?

And we laugh.

It's not easy to explain how a life can accept to give life by separating it from itself. She tries...But her eyes tell me more than words can.

I'm not a father, I'm not a mother. I can't understand everything ... Not with words ...Not this time.

Every day she arrives home destroyed. Happy, for the two, one, perhaps three new babies in the world. If not six ... When she gets home she asks her husband to get her a beer. Each of these first breaths is very tiring for the obstetrician. Childbirth shakes her too– for better or for worse.

She remains serious for thirty seconds and then laughs again. And it makes me laugh. She tells me she loves babies because they're not human yet. When they become human and call themselves children, she can't stand them anymore. Can't stand children!

Hers is still a young marriage. Now she doesn't want children. But can you imagine no children! One imagines her future full of children and animals ... And perhaps beer.

"But not now ... Now I have no maternity instinct ... Now I can't stand children!"

But she loves babies.

And then I stop laughing.

Every day she arrives home destroyed.

For new babies in the world, or for assisting women on a difficult journey. Neither beautiful nor fun. A very heavy thing they don't normally do, and she doesn't do lightly either.

At twelve weeks this baby that will be, is called a fetus. But it's a word you use to protect yourself, just in case ... It's not easy... Now she becomes even more serious. She has a strong, direct gaze, without hesitation. She's a professional.

And she's a professional who does not approve of anti-abortionists. Even while she was studying she knew that this would be part of her job. "If you don't like it, you don't do that job ... It's too easy to become anti-abortion ... Wash your hands ... This thing will be done away with ...

Women will continue to have abortions ... What you can do is protect this person and make sure that this choice does not become a tragedy ... I think my job is to assist them in this difficult journey ... "

When a woman arrives, and within ninety days she has made the decision that ninety-one will not be, she has chosen to assist her. And if she cries, laughs, she's alone, she has company, it seems superficial, she tries not to judge.

She immediately repeats... and hammers the words into my brain ... "NO ... I DO NOT JUDGE!"

"My work is beautiful and very ugly at the same time, and when you choose to do a job like this you choose to assist women, not judge them."

It's no longer funny. Maybe it never was. She claims she didn't get much from her mother! But I definitely have a ballsy woman in front of me. Self-confident.

Acutely sensitive.

The IVG (voluntary termination of pregnancy) is part of her job, and according to her, if you do this job, you get the complete package. It's not beautiful or funny; it's a very heavy thing that she does not do lightly, but her job is to assist women in this difficult course, while the doctor intervenes ...

Most women are a little worse off before than after. There are those who cry, those who are remote, those who laugh hysterically.

And she is there to assist.

"Women who have abortions can become wonderful mothers ... It just didn't happen at the right time ...And when that happens ... I'll always be there to assist ... "

And maybe she will cry.
With a new baby in hand ...
And his first breath.

She will cry together with a woman born only for that man. The father. And a man born only for that woman. The mother.

Maybe she arrived without support. The support of a very small country with an even smaller flock. The support of those who didn't have the courage to make the same choices.

For love...
The only true love.

....

Biella is halfway between Turin and Milan. On the map it is slightly offset from the two, as if it wanted to be the apex of a triangle. This upward position is the beginning of a complete cluster fuck. If it were in the middle of the road that connects Turin to Milan, it would simply be a convenient exit off the A4

motorway. But no! If you want to go by car from Milan to Biella you have to go out halfway on this road, where you won't find the Biella sign, but Carisio (Carisio ???) ...
Having taken this exit, you'll then spend a half hour crossing rice fields with speed cameras hidden under water and traffic lights, placed where they could have put two comfortable French roundabouts.

Do you want to try it by train?

The train that leaves from Biella is particularly nice. It is one of the most modern. The station is small and perfectly acceptable. There's also a beautiful fountain in front to dive when Italy makes in the final stages of European or World Cup.

It's a pity that...The nice train stops in Santhia (Santhia ???) or in Novara. The first in the direction of Turin, the second in the direction of Milan. Once we arrive in one of these two stations we have to do one of two things, inversely proportional:

Thing Number 1: Run!

The switch-over has been designed to allow one train to arrive and the next one to leave allowing passengers to get off, stretch their legs, light a cigarette, get to the platform, look at a girl's ass waiting for the next train ...But ... we don't talk about our train being 10 minutes late??? Once we get off the cute little train all hell breaks loose ... Which platform do we have to go to? ... Slowly, don't push ... Ohhh, who touched my ass? Run...

Thing Number 2: Wait!

The switch-over has been designed to allow one train to arrive and the next to leave allowing passengers to get off, stretch their legs, light a cigarette, get to the platform, wait for the best time to ... But ten minutes late for the arriving train. And thirty? And it's January, it's freezing cold. The track is uncovered. Scarves, beards, the desire to conduct human relationships, the desire to live freeze. The second train is on its way ... and it's full! Full of warm human beings, with their jackets parked comfortably in the overhead bin, and laptops open between their legs. If they have a free seat next to them, they make you feel like a beggar who's allowed a stay in a room the size of a purple monopoly box where they put an hotel.

I have to record some songs somewhere for some band. Definitely the group and the song of my life, because I no longer remember one or the other. I get on the train that would have taken me from Biella to Milan, stopping in Novara. Destiny will decide whether I will switch-over at thing number 1 or 2.

We arrive in Novara.

Thing Number 2: Wait.

The train arrives from Turin to Milan. It's a train with at least a dozen cars. I hop up. I'm lucky, it's not peak time, there are some places here and there. I do as everyone does, I look for a free seat in front of another free seat. Those who come after me will have to look at me and humble themselves as if I were the owner of monopoly, including the aqueduct and electric company.

But at some point I see him ...

I recognize him ... He conveys peace even while traveling by train. His stories have always managed to lead me to questions or laughter, like when he told about finding a worm in a plant. What better company for an hour of travel ...

by the way... What did the woodworm taste like?

"I'll tell you... ... It tasted like wood! "

Simple isn't it?

- Track 2 -

Enough, today I'm going to ask, today I'm going to ask how much it costs.

Spring is coming, the days are cloudless. Below the house the number of cyclists increases, the passage of motorcycles increases, and the noise in the sky also increases.
Every time a bike passes, I keep doing what I'm doing.
But every time a Cessna or any other ultralight sub-brand passes by, I thumb my nose at them.

Today I'm going to ask how much it costs to get a pilot's license ...

... and it costs too much!

That is, if one has five or six salaries combined, he can afford the whim; but I. I have a good computer, it should be powerful enough to ... Let's look at the features ...Yeah ! Search engine, two clicks, enter. After two days I can learn to fly over my house. I spent what I would have spent on a regular Saturday night buying a friend a beer. A used flight simulator and joystick.

I spend a couple of hours setting up and installing all these gadgets. Power up and, there they are: the Cessna, all the discount sub-brands of ultralights, and also the Airbus, the Boeing; nooooo, even the Top Gun Jet. Really !

There are all the airports in the world. And then there's the one where I went to ask for the license.

I want to fly over my house, but I'm methodical.

When I buy something, before I start using it, I always read the instructions.

Oh my God: flight lessons, codes, checklists, terminologies, aerodynamics, radio communications, etc. I'll have to study for days. I'm excited, I'll become a pilot.

I start flying lessons and learn take-off. Easy, put the plane on the runway, keep it straight, increase the speed, push the joystick back ...

... You're flying.

Lesson completed!

Then stay in the air, turn right, turn left.

The landing begins. Easy, see the track, keep it straight, decrease the throttle ...... and as you get closer you see that the track is slightly to the right. Then you turn slightly to the right and suddenly the track is way to the left. Then you turn quickly to the left and suddenly you don't see it anymore. You turn your head to the right, and you see the refrigerator. You turn your head to the left and see the cabinet with the liquor. You begin to think that you will have to buy eighteen more monitors that rotate around you 360 degrees. You don't remember which button is used to stop the radio from telling you that ...

... That you crashed!

I learned how to take off with a light aircraft in a few minutes. It took me a few days of extra minutes to land.

Then you get a hang of it after a few weeks, when the landings nearly start to be perfect.

If you haven't landed on the runway, but in the parallel lawn next to it, that's okay, as long as the radio folks haven't noticed.
And don't we don't need prove I'm Boeing?

I learn to take–off. Easy, put the plane on the runway, keep it straight, increase the speed, push the joystick back ...
And ... And why doesn't it start? How the hell do you start the engine? What are all these buttons? I am methodical, remember? So ... I press them all! But the plane doesn't move.

Checklist. I learn the checklist. A long list of things to do to get my Boeing going. Each step is essential. It's essential to check each point before moving on to the next one. I remember that movie with Tom Hanks, that true story of astronauts who if they don't follow the checklist step by step meticulously, they won't go home. Here. It all makes sense. Now I understand. With the checklist my plane takes off.

... Don't ask about the landing, ok?

Every morning, at breakfast, I prepare the checklist.
I need to stay focused. Above all I also need to understand that I'm moving forward. Tick after tick. Centimeter by centimeter. Slow, but forward. There are moments where it seems to me that nothing is moving forward. I only see insurmountable problems. I only see things to be solved and which have no solution.

Then I look at the checklist.

I look at the sheet:

~~Study 121 to 140~~
~~Try starting from 33 instead of 15~~
~~Record in multitake~~
~~Call Ste for Friday evening~~

Study 141 to 160

I've already completed 140 pages of that book! Incredible. That book was too big to open when it arrived. Too big and too much English to be able to absorb quickly. That book is an exam. That exam is perhaps the beginning of my new life, and if I don't start it, I no longer know which way to turn.

And then a method. I watch it for a few minutes.
I decide how much time I want to study. 2 months?
Good ! I divide it by 60. No! I divide it by 50.
I know myself, and there will be ten days like today where I don't want to do anything; where I'm a little down; where I don't think I'll go where I want to go. I also budgeted those days.
The other fifty days I have to study twenty pages.
Twenty times fifty is a thousand. One thousand is twice the number of pages in the book. After reading the book twice, I'll have understood!

Two months:
I have already done 121 to 140. It's the second time !

Checklist.

Every day it helps me understand where I am.
Every day it helps me understand where I am and where I'm not.

Today I cleared all the guidelines ahead of schedule.
I have a clear conscience. I can have a nice flight.

Take off.

Now I have learned.

There's my house. There's the river ...
Then beyond ...

I wait a moment for them to pass by.

Come on ... Let's do it ...

Today I'm going to crash into Mont Blanc.

"I miss a lot of little things. His resting his forehead on mine to give me strength. His playing cards; there was no way to beat him in Scopa or Briscola. Then he loved to go mushrooming.
When he couldn't find any, he collected feathers! "

So she told me about her father.

She's tall, blonde and beautiful, and has such a strong gaze, that if someone thought of approaching her to woo her, with a glance they would find themselves frosted like an icicle in a winter freezer. No ! They didn't put me in the microwave to defrost.
I met her for a much more profound reason.

Video games !

I've been playing it since I was a kid. I have a physiological decline in summer, but when autumn arrives I feel the call. The dusty console looks at me. I turn it on just for a moment to check if the cables behind haven't been disconnected by the frequent passage of cats, wild hide–and–seek fights behind the furniture. That moment is crucial!

The next day I'm already looking for second–hand video games, the ones that have recently come out and that someone has decided to sell at half price for both.
Days in which I said to myself, one more game, just one more game, and then it's time for dinner. But did I have lunch?
Then there are the games where I suck. I'm just not there. I try, but as soon as I put my mug online, they slaughter me with punches or machine guns. I imagine some child on the other side of the world who laughs while blowing my head off with a sniper rifle. Or racing games. My position depends only on the number of players online at that time. Don't worry though. It will almost always be next to last. The next day I'll try again, and then the next several months, and for as long as I remember.

Its part of the game. Someone has to win, and everyone does against me.

But I enjoy it.

Today I removed the dust and I have all the latest updates, too bad they are the unplayable ones from the last century. The time has come to put them on online antiques markets. It's also the year of the console. Staying on the penultimate version for three years is the right time to wait for the price drop of the last one. But now it's been four. My old rig did her job well. The evenings at Guitar Hero with friends were countless, but now the new Rock Band is out; then the disc drawer doesn't open at the first stroke; then .... Well I want to change it, ok?

Between the purchase of the new one and the sale of the old one, a hidden part of my personality comes to life, an add-On inherited from my mother:
the south italian merchant who won't be fooled in any way. A very exhausting period of bargaining and swearing in unknown languages begins, a historical period where the best of my character is displayed.
There are always those who try to lower the price of my goods by belittling them, and they end up embarrassing themselves. Or I answer the various "TRADE WITH ..." without even trying to be polite. In exchange for my console, they try to dump the most pathetic objects on me, and absolutely out of the videogame subset: electric chainsaws, vintage lego cubes, canary feeders, anthropology books.

I'm nursing an acid stomach when I receive yet another message; this time it's a person unaware of this underground infighting between gamers. She's a "normal" person. She lives in the area, and would like to buy my console table for her son. At the first contact she offers me the most absurd thing that has ever happened to me for my online ads: wants to give me the money requested in the ad.

There was a moment of silence in my conscience, I still remember it vividly. Then my NO! For a child, my console with a crappy drawer was not suitable.
I imagined the child fumbling with 2 screwdrivers in ninja mode in search of the perfect position to unlock the jammed

mechanism (which was what I did). Then get started with endless swearing and blasphemy.

I proposed a more suitable console on offer in a nearby shopping center... And I forgot about it.

But she didn't!

A few days later, while I continue my struggles with the crazed barters (before reaching a compromise between tweedledee and tweedledum three generations of consoles can be eliminated) I receive a message. She discovered that I wrote a book, and she would like to buy it in exchange for my honesty, after meeting in a cafe. Another moment of silence ...

I bet you now think: what luck (you didn't use this word ...) now he meets her and ...I, on the other hand, who's malice is the envy of no one, on that particular occasion was thinking: should I use a car to deliver a book that can be ordered online? To a mother? With this cold I have to leave the house? I try to politely derail the request by directing her to a library in town.

I fail miserably.

With Great Enthusiasm on one hand and "Little Dreams" on the other, I meet her. Mom is tall, blonde and beautiful. The conversation is intelligent and its energy is particularly strong. Imagine something like Mrs. Rottermaier while on vacation. Her gaze is strong even when smiling. This prompts me to ask her questions.

I learn from her that she has a son. To make a living she takes care of small children. She reads a lot of books ...

... and in a short time she saw her marriage collapse without doing anything to prevent it... let her father die ...
...decided to suspend the birth of the second child.

"I am sorry for one death .... Not for the other! "
I watch her carefully. I listen to her and have a hard time keeping judgments at bay..

Despite my efforts only three words predominate.

Euthanasia, Abortion, Divorce.

She's tall, blonde and beautiful. To make a living, she takes care of small children.

Divorce, Euthanasia, Abortion.

I visualize someone in a corner preparing a nice bonfire to tie the witch to. Yeah, you can find some wood behind the garden, alcohol and the lighter are in the garage. Just wait ten minutes, then I'll come and help you.

Abortion, Divorce, Euthanasia.

Voices from hell say they are furnishing a beautiful suite down there. To make a living, she takes care of small children. She's tall, blonde and beautiful. Video games. Wait, I get it. She's the ultimate monster?

STOP

I pause everything.

How deeply have I meditated on each of these three words? Or how little did I really? Tall Blonde and Beautiful ???

nooooo

Euthanasia, Abortion, Divorce: three GIANT words !!! I listen to those.

Her parents had two daughters, one of 16 and one of 12. Their economic situation was a disaster. They decide they can't have a third child. They love each other.

They make the difficult decision together. The oldest knows, the youngest doesn't.

The oldest gets engaged. Is happy. After 4 years she gets married. After a great deal of complications, a son is born.

Her father, the man who collected feathers, fell ill at 58. She, daughter, wife and happy mother, is 32.

Cancer.

It spread very fast. The doctors are merciless, telling her that the death would occur within two months. He would die naturally, with a lot of pain.

But he didn't know! He lasted 6 months.

In six months, the blue eyes became dull and watery. From a robust 200 lbs. to a spectral 90.

He ends up in one of those beautiful and colorful hospital rooms. The oncology ward. The more the daughter sees the brightly colored wards, the more she understands that death is approaching.

Her mother is unable to accompany him for 8 hours of chemo. She's alone and wants to take care of it alone. She keeps her husband at a distance too. He no longer pays attention to his grandson.

She watches her father eat like a lion during the 3 days after chemo. Chemo gives you the munchies and they put sweets in the room. His energy returns after eating, he listens to music.

Hopes are raised. They end quickly!

Fourth month. The daughter does not give up. On television there is talk of a miraculous scorpion poison in Cuba, it would block tumor growth and have a painkilling effect. With 3 other desperate and unknown families, found on the internet, she organizes the mission. Medical records on the way to Cuba ... Vials of poison arrive. Exchanges take place at the airport. The climate is very surreal. She feels like a junkie buying a hit.

The poison works. It has a pain-relieving effect. The tumor does not grow. But it had grown enough! It's so big that it's too late!

Fifth month. He moves very little. He no longer feeds. Eats only ice.

They decide to take him home. Opioid medicines induce hallucinations; he's aware of it, and with his inevitable humor he jokes with the hallucinations in front of his daughter.

There is a strange energy in the air. There is an awareness that no one should have to live. He understands it's the last week!

One last game of cards with the two daughters. He's light as a feather, smells different, doesn't have a mustache and doesn't eat, but he smiles. He doesn't even lose this time. On their way home the daughters can't stop smiling about it. The father always wins.

The next day the agony begins. The "He will naturally die with much pain" has come.

A doctor proposes an alternative to waiting for everything to run its course: asks his father if he would rather fall asleep. With a mix of drugs and morphine, he would fall asleep very peacefully, would never be conscious again. If he had decides yes, there would be a maximum life expectancy of 5 days, as he would no longer eat and drink. They accept, but the last word is up to him.

"How do you feel?" ... So tired ... "Would you like to sleep? Have a deep sleep? " ... Yes.

"If you have something to say do it now" She doesn't remember what she and her father said to each other, she never asked her mother and sister.

The doctor went in alone. Five minutes after the shot he was already asleep: "It was all so fast! "
A syringe of morphine is left in the fridge, to be used in the case of evident severe pain. It would be over 10 minutes later.

As the doctor leaves the house, she advises us to start organizing the funeral arrangements.

I listen to her. After two days, apply the syringe. She has very labored breathing. It's safe. She's suffering!

"I injected him and he fell asleep on the sofa immediately. After taking several very long breaths, he died 10 minutes later with my mom by his side. I didn't cry.

" At that moment the marriage also dies. He respected that she didn't involve him such "private" pain. She wanted this, but this wasn't the best for their relationship. They've remained on excellent terms. The son is loved by both of them, but their love has flown away.

They separated. Divorce.

After some time she starts a new affair. He's also separated. He has an older daughter. There's an understanding. Everything works. Coexistence begins. He, she, two children.

After a year, happiness becomes "Maybe" happiness. A 'maybe' dictated by various misunderstandings. Normal adjustments? Maybe !

In the midst of it all 'maybe' a great certainty arrives. She gets pregnant.
It's discovered in the eighth week. She decides to keep it.
The tenth week they book a clinic visit. During those fifteen days her companion loses the 'maybe.' Zero joy!

He's already got an older daughter. His ex has another child on the way. Discussions. Doubts. In short, he says NO. Discussions. Not wanted but unavoidable.
Discussions. Distances.

Alone! Alone again this time!

Hospital again. This time she wanted her partner close, however ... He wasn't there. The words that came out in the discussions were too fierce. Too intense, and they couldn't be held inside any longer. Pride and pain. Silence...Or maybe it was more convenient this way ...

Maybe.

She didn't even seek help from her mother, despite knowing that she had terminated a pregnancy in the past. She had done it for economic reasons, but this time there were no health, money or malformation problems.

If she had talked to her she would have helped her. She didn't want to! "I don't want forgiveness !!! "

She wouldn't do it again today!

She's tall, blonde and beautiful, and has such a strong gaze, that if someone thought of approaching her to woo her, with a glance they would find themselves frosted like an icicle in a winter freezer. She works with children who would be the age of her second child ... if he were born.

She sees them grow. She helps them grow.

She doesn't want forgiveness. To tell the truth, I still haven't figured out if ...

... Forgiveness?

I give up. Thanks for waiting. Have you found the alcohol and the lighter? Put them back in the garage after ...I'm not coming.

I prefer to listen to her talk a little more about her first child. He's very happy. You know? He has a particular passion. No one ever taught him .. he collects feathers.

- Track 16 -

Justice. Where is this justice which everyone rinses their mouths?
Where is it? Is it on the right, is it on the left? Why don't I see it?

That beautiful woman, blindfolded, with a sword in one hand and
a scale in the other. How does she know who is right from who is
wrong if she can't see us?

How does everyone know what's right and what's wrong?
How do they have no doubts? Even before the TV news ends
they've already understood everything. They would never do that.
They would never forgive.

Instead, I always have doubts. I feel like the devil's advocate, and
the devil is squeezing my balls.

I'm not talking about thieves and killers. They're the most
recognizable.

But the others, have I always recognized them?

Those who shake your hand.

Those who look you straight in the eye.

Those who smile at you.

Those who are polite.

Those who are not.

Those that are studied.

Those that are studied and even learned.

Those who pamper your soul and are touched by you.

Those that consider you the winner and pull the chariot for you.

You believe in handshakes. You believe in looks and tears. You would never lie. You wouldn't be able to look someone you're about to hit in the eye.

Besides, real life isn't always fair. What you saw is not always true.

You work for someone, and the money doesn't arrive. That money is the difference between red or black in the bank ... and if the bank calls, it calls you, not someone else.

You're in line and someone cuts into the line. They would never cheat, and then they cheat. Someone at the top holds you back to promote the friend, the relative, the butcher. What's the real truth?

Someone is responsible and wrong. He admits his mistake ...

Then someone is never wrong. You were wrong for them.

Someone muddies your name to avoid theirs being examined.

Some take it for granted that it's normal to lie. And if you get angry, they smile. If you lose your temper they stay polite. They are the form of their substance. Liquid. Fits into a container! They are calm. Educated in an educated world. They smile. They're in control of what they do ... And you feel like throwing a punch!

I read in the ancient psalms of adversaries who were outraged, and in the meantime no sign, no prophet.

Until?

Shouldn't justice be a free gift? A gift of man's nature?
Because the blindfolded woman gets paid by lawyers. Time.
Anxious and more injustice.

Until?

When the blindfold is removed will justice really be justice? If I'm wrong, I'm punished, but if they made a mistake, you don't smile for them anymore.

If man were truly man, justice would not be needed.

If the man were truly a man I wouldn't want to punch someone!

How does everyone know what is right and what is wrong?

Why do they have no doubts?

He has a castle. The castle is on a corner ridge. The corner ridge is on a peak.

The misanthrope's peak is the place where, you may have guessed, the misanthrope lives.

You can't see it from a distance or even up close.
You have to know its path before reaching it.

Around him live a few others: those of the club. He's a member of the club, but he hates it. He's obliged to be member if he wants to have a corner, and a corner castle, on a peak. He hates the club. He always manages to invent new offerings. If you have your own castle, and a corner of the peak, you must pay an offering for the castle and an offering also for the corner of the peak. He hates the club, but he's obligated to be a part of it.

Our Hard Haid Moe in flesh and blood has a frown like him, but he has no white beard, hat, and bored dog around.

I know his path by heart, and I also know his frowning face by heart.

I warned him. He waits for me, but I know that as soon as I cross the threshold of the castle, thinking of me approaching, he'll be agitated and uncomfortable. He doesn't trust humanity, but he knows I hate the club too. He also knows that unlike him I have decided to stay in the middle, I have decided to stay amongst those others. Without the need to understand them anymore. Without the need to change them anymore.

I know his initial discomfort at each meeting. His shotgun is always loaded with anxiety and panic attacks, but we've already discussed it in the past. We have already clashed, attacked, defended and clarified. Many times I have not understood him, but I've never judged him. You can speak freely with me.

With the curtains on the windows closed. The intercom that rings shocks him, and with those others ... outside.

Our Hard Haid Moe does not need science books to understand that he's a misanthrope. His book is written easier than Leopardi's. He keeps away from others. He seeks solitude and peace away from others.

Mr. Moe and I are very different. Right now both of us are out of money, and if there are dues to pay... they'll wait. But if he has three bucks, he goes to shop at the mini-markets where the mini-mountain dwellers go shopping. Antisocial. If I have two bucks, I go to the bigger ones, with many people and spend more than I can afford.

We both have free time. Blessing and curse. Both with or without little work. More than the uncertainty of tomorrow, there is a precise uncertainty for the early afternoon.

I've sought this free time. Not him ! Yet he has feelings of guilt. Not me ! It should be the other way around.

In the last five years both of us have run out of cheese. Before it was over, I tied my shoes and started running in search of any more cheese reserves. I read it in a book, so it's right, isn't it? Instead, he waited for the cheese reserves to finish, without even looking for his shoes to tie. Nobody blamed anyone else. No one had stolen the cheese from us. We just ate it. I keep running even though it seems to me that I've already searched all the streets. But he no longer wants to go out.

We both feel uncomfortable with all this free time we can spend chatting. But he also has feelings of guilt, I don't.

At first the desire to go out decreases. Lack of money leads you to isolation. You begin to refuse some drinks, some dinners with friends. After a while, the others no longer call you.

When he lost his job, the club helped him for two years.

Redundancy fund. He had never had a problem getting a job before. It just happened. He didn't even know what a resume was. He hasn't sent one in two years.

Sooner or later the money will come. It will happen.

It all seems easy right? You've all already reached your conclusions. One crashes and sooner or later something happens. And the other one is fucked. But that's not quite the case. Because I know Hard Haid, and he's no worse than the others.

He's kept his nose to the grindstone for more than twenty years. He has dreamed and touched dreams that most of you, including me, will probably never touch. Musician. Lyricist. He didn't become a rock star. He is a rock star.

Hard Haid Moe has been on television. In crowded plazas, with people who were thrilled to see and admire him.
And who also listened to his music too. There were friends everywhere. When he played and was famous they were all brothers. Now that he's back among them, in the middle of the club, like a brother ... He doesn't see anyone anymore.

I try to talk about it, to not to forget, because it's right not to forget.

Mr Moe, like me and you, is selfish! He did something that made others feel good, but above all it was good for him.

When this something stopped feeling good, he put it aside ... And he was put aside.

He has no desire to work. He looks at me and tells me serenely that he no longer wants to do shit. I understand. He's true to himself. He's always been honest with others as well.

He worked on his dreams for many years with others who contributed nothing. Despite a full day job, Mr. Moe arrived on time to rehearsals, but the others often didn't ... They were playing the slot machines. He changed musicians often, always looking them in the eye. Being a rock star is not a lucky spin on the slot machines. It's hard. It takes commitment. Consistency. Desire.

Twenty years, and he's always been a rock star with the right personnel. Changing them every time they disappointed him. If he didn't find the right people, he wouldn't play. Why start something we don't like from the start? Things we don't like.

His father says he should take any job. Maybe he's right. But how do you accept just 'anything' after twenty years as a rock star?

He's strong. He's a charge of dynamite when he understands what he wants to do. But now that he no longer wants to be a rock star what does he want to do? He does look for jobs. He'd also accept anything .. He asked a around here and there. But deep down he hopes he doesn't find a job. Not before knowing what it is. If only he knew what he wanted to do.

He suffers from insomnia. Sometimes sleep is aided by a bottle, but he doesn't know if got into bed or tripped over it.

He's Mr Moe, and he's selfish, like me and you. He doesn't like living with a shotgun full of anxiety and panic. He always wants to be in control of what happens. He never wants to lose control.

He entrusts himself to an expert hypnotist. One of the famous ones, not the best one. A rock star in his field. After meeting him he won't be able to pay many club dues. He's goes back to the castle without a solution. He's unhypnotizable. He doesn't lose control. He doesn't want to lose it, and so he doesn't.

He goes to other specialists. The answer they give 90% of the time: it all comes from the family. Sure ! Every rock star has a family.
He can't stand his, but he already knew this while he was waiting for those who played the slot machines. He is music and his father never bought a record. Hard Haid Moe can't understand anyone who doesn't listen to music. Who doesn't turn on the car radio while driving. Even though he hates music now, he keeps listening to it. But his family doesn't ... And he can't stand it.

Trust doesn't have to be earned, it just has to be given, and he
trusted yet another specialist. The sign read: Psychiatrist.
Only after many payments it was discovered that he was not.
Today this genius earns his living by piercing.

He can speak freely with me. With the window curtains closed.
With an intercom that shocks him if it rings, and with those
others ... outside.

We pour ourselves a second glass of the wine I brought to my
favorite misanthrope.

While he was a rock star he lived at least three lives.
And also we smile at this. We understand each other.

Electrician, and as soon as he left school, convinced he'd do it the
rest of his life. The eagerness to make money soon appeared.
But the electrician is called to the military. Aside from the loaded
shotgun of anxiety and panic, he never wanted to touch weapons.
The club finds a place for him doing social work, to help children.

My asocial misanthrope friend loves social work.

He's always been hungry to help. But then he saw another type of
hunger. That of finding the guilty in complex family situations.
The hunger of morbid social workers he saw working in the next
room. He's not only disappointed, but something inside of him
dies. As well as outside. The suicide of innocents cannot be
metabolized.

Hard Haid Moe stops here. I remain still. He... With all due respect
for his role, we'll leave the talk-show cameras out of these pages
for now.

Let's move on, weren't there three lives? Right.

 "Look, they need someone where I work" Sooner or later the
money will come. It will happen. It happened. While he was
dreaming and living as a rock star.

A company of about twenty employees. Women. Plus one. Man.
Him: "I'm going to retire here." A warehouse with a lot of
downtime to be able to write songs, but with a fixed monthly fee
to pay for dreams. He doesn't just work for a couple of days.
It does this for ten years.

He does it for ten years !!!

And in ten years his songs arrive simultaneously on television.
On those stages where others looked at him admiringly.
Some even listened to his songs, as well as watching them.

He doesn't give up work! Ten years !!! I know Hard Haid and he's
no worse than the others. Although he's already a rock star, he
hasn't stopped working yet. He hasn't even stopped dreaming.

It's the job that leaves him. Bankrupt company.

I have sought this free time. Not him. Yet he has feelings of guilt.
Not me.

We talk about friends, loves. Of women ... of men.

Women up to their twenties ... After only the sufferings of love.
He doesn't like sex for its own sake. He needs to prove
something. But he has a serious problem. He would like to
understand who he is and who he is not. He would like to
understand who he is and who he is not before falling in love with
someone, who maybe is just a lark; and then leaves. But he
remains instead. And he feels bad.

Suffering wins by playing with ambiguity. He would have
preferred to be "who he's not". And in spite of himself he
conquers the "who he's not". But conquering and loving are very
different things.

We pour ourselves a third glass ...

Mr. Moe and I are very different. We are both penniless right now. If bills arrive to pay, they'll wait! I feel his initial discomfort at each meeting ... But the discomfort always eases long before the end of the meeting. He knows that many times I haven't understood him, but I've never judged him.

Let's talk about faith, about my best friend. Maybe I'm an optimist so I search for the road directed toward miracles. Then "ask and it will be given to you" worked a lot for me.

He doesn't pray because he doesn't like to ask ... According to him, the devil does not exist ... "There is only God, she's a woman and she's evil!" We laugh ... Could God be a woman ... I never thought about it, I don't want to now ... "But it's in front of God that I would like to marry, when and with whom it's all a great, ah ..." Mr Moe takes out a pearl ... "In Italy now only gays want to get married"

We laugh like two who have lost some kind of club card.
I would like to get married ...
Not him!

I'm in his castle.

The castle is on the corner.

The corner is on a peak.

We say goodbye...I have to keep running even if it seems to me that I have already searched all the roads. But he no longer wants to go out. He doesn't know what he's waiting for. But the illumination which he's destined for awaits him in his castle. And when it comes, he'll know how to pour all his commitment and rockstar energy into it.

He waits...

In his Play-Doh castle,

He's the king of the world!

Once a year I receive his call. He's about to arrive in Italy.
I haven't been his colleague for a long time, but every time he goes to work for my old company, there's always a case of beer for me and a bottle of Becherovka. Followed by giant slaps on the back, sincere laughter, and then we go to dinner where we drink and eat as if there was no tomorrow. After dinner, we hug, bye, see you next year.

His name is Vladimir.

He told me a lot about what Czechoslovakia was like before and how life changed when the two nations separated. When I went to Prague he gave me two surprises. First, he introduced me to one of the best beers in the world, Velvet, second; he chased a police car. He was calm and I didn't understand why, but once he pulled over he introduced me to who was driving that car ... His daughter.

Whenever there are European or World Cups, our message exchanges during matches are inevitable. As we exchange messages, we send each other a picture while opening a beer.

We're very good friends Vladimir and I.

But yet...

We were doing a job in Slovakia, and there were other technicians with us, including those, the more precise ones.

The Swiss.
Working with the Swiss is very easy, they are methodical, they leave little or nothing to chance, and if you stick to the rules you will hardly have problems. If we add the German word to the

Swiss word, you will have even less. We are working with a Swiss German colleague, a guy with the most dour character. The kind that if something goes wrong hardly smiles, and since we're technicians, and we're technicians who work to solve problems, there's always something that goes wrong. Vladimir and I are a team, we've worked together many times, and we're used to coming out of the most difficult situations with a smile.

We arrive at the hotel, where everyone has their room booked. It's our first night after a difficult day with conflicts erupting on all sides. It's me, Vladimir, the Swiss–German, and another particularly unpleasant technician who comes from god knows where. There should be four rooms, but someone forgot to book a room for Vladimir. The girl from the hotel assures us that each of the other three rooms still has two single beds, so ...
So Vladimir looks at us.

And I'm a coward again!

It's the second time in my life that I leave my friend to think about myself first. The first time happened when four of us are taken to barracks where we don't know anyone. They can't guarantee us a bed for the night and we're prepared for the worst. All for one, one for all. As soon as we walk down the corridor, I notice a free cot in a passing room: "Is that free?. "Yeah"! And I throw my backpack on it.

My three mates look at me perplexed, but why, aren't we a team? Yes, but I was scared and I wasn't strong enough, and I stayed in a room with strangers. They wanted to scare us and they succeeded, because then they all slept, and all three stayed together. The next day, rightly, they ignored me.

And this time?

I think about the fact that the day has been long and I don't want to share a bathroom with anyone, and ... and five seconds go by that ... That the Swiss–German offers Vladimir his room. The one with the most unpleasant character offers the solution, not the friend, that is, me.

It's already happened twice. How many times have I judged others for similar gestures? But yet...You never know each other well enough when you're truly cornered.

They say there's no two without three.

Vladimir forgave me without ever remembering the episode, and I want to remember it now ...

... let them talk!

I snore. There are situations where I snore more and situations where I snore less, but I snore always.
And there are times that I snore so loudly that I can hear myself snore too, and it wakes me up as if to tell me: there is a limit to everything!

Since they say that God creates them and then pairs them, my cat snores too, and almost always too; almost because sometimes he wakes up because I snore too much, and he paws my face to make me stop. He's snoring right now too! He takes advantage of the fact that I'm awake.

And Munnè is also snoring. Munnè stands for garbage. I've always called him that and he always replied that I'm garbage too. He has the manners of a bear walking into a crystal shop. Looks at an ornament, thinks about touching it, and has already broken it. He's arranging the pieces and has already broken the window. He says he's sorry but the clerk has already freaked out.

He's a bear, and he's also a sleepy bear. But how can he be so sleepy? He slept all night, breathing heavily. He snores like a beast. And it's an ugly snore, the ugliest kind there is. The kind where the snoring stops suddenly. If you're there, you take a breath: relieved that he's stopped, alright now I can sleep a little better, but ...

But now he's not breathing ...

He can't breathe anymore ... Oh God he's dead ...

And suddenly with a single snort he slaps you in the face with all the noise that was missing before; as if he had wanted to accumulate the decibels for a single, well-defined roar. Then continues. You don't sleep well at night next to someone like that. Yet he's sleepy. Is tired. Can't focus on work. He says he doesn't sleep well, but man, are you pissing us off!

No !

He wakes up agitated, sweaty, with a very sharp tachycardia and anguish: the sense of suffocation. It's the weight, it's the work, the stress, it's whatever, but the anguish does not abate. Indeed, night after night, the anguish gets worse. In the morning, headache, sore throat and gets angry at work; can't concentrate.

Stop !!! "Stop joking. I really don't sleep well at night! "

Start the visits:
The heart, the lungs.
Then other visits:
The mouth, the nose, the throat.
Then other visits:

The sleep specialist.

They place sensors on his scalp, face, chest, arms, legs ... And on a finger. Brain activity, eye movements, heart rate, pressure. How much oxygen does he have in his blood, how he moves while snoring and even how much air passes into the nose while breathing.

The result is that now that we're about to sleep in the room together, after having partyed all day, Munnè decides to turn into a scuba diver. A strap under the ears, one on the forehead, and a transparent mask in the middle. The tube starts from the mask and ends up in a machine that occupies half of the bedside table. He's a little ashamed of it, but for us he's the least of our problems. We're still sending flowers to the clerk's wife.

Sleep Apnea.

A syndrome in which the patient's breathing stops one or more times during sleep. The breaks can last a few seconds, up to three minutes. Till death.

God creates them and then pairs them and they have mated for many years. And for many years he has been mating with the hand of God. He's a pastor. A man who marries, who baptizes, who preaches, who takes care of his flock. Drives away wolves and raises lambs. He's a pastor I've known for a long time. We've talked a lot about how he came to faith. He's not the son of pastors. No nepotism. It's the result of research, travel, mistakes, experiments. He's the product of tests with other religions, he's the son of reading and curiosity, he's the son of touching where you must not touch, and he was also the son of ... er ... the son of many doubts. But when he was chosen, the doubts vanished, forever, and he gave up everything to follow his vocation, to follow his Father! A friend with whom I love to talk, joke, learn, and reflect. Sometimes I don't share what he tells me, and he doesn't share what I tell him. I'm not a member of a church, and therefore I'm not a member of your church either.
But if one day I really had to choose one, I think I would choose his.

But he doesn't ask anymore!

He learned to respect my personal relationship with our Best Friend, and my pseudo-religious anarchy.

I really like it when we confront each other. He's so certain, I'm so
certain, and then so uncertain. 'And then again of course, and
then no; but if then' ... And like a child asking questions, and
listening to the answers with his mouth open. And then again no,
I don't agree with that. But this yes. And then we smile.
And then he either blesses me, or hugs me, or he recommends a
song.

They are those friends you never see. Really never. Those you
maybe hear from a couple of times a year if all goes well. But
when you hear from them you're really happy, because you're
feeling like true friends and real men.

True because I'll always remember his eyes. He had invited me to
a concert, and I had always liked his church concerts.
There weren't those memorized unlistenable dirges that I
couldn't stand. There were guitars, keyboards, microphones,
amplifiers. In short, there was some healthy Rock in the church.
So!

A mass more lively than what I was used to. Almost similar to the
gospel ones I had seen on television, where they smile while they
sing and pray, and I don't understand if I have to laugh or if I have
to pray. And in the end I laugh as I pray, and as I listen to music.
It's cool !

But first of all ...

His eyes.

He was preaching, and his sermons don't have a timetable; they
start when they start and end when they have to end.
There is little preparation. They're almost improvised Jazz
sermons, and they're inspired.

There was talk of mourning. He had to lighten the burden of someone, someone of his flock. To do it... He talked about Sara.

Sara is four and a half months old. For two months the faces of mum and dad have become only shadows. She smiles, she smiles a lot. It's the only language she has already learned to communicate with her parents. Those who feed her, change her diaper, put her to sleep. She smiles, they smile ... And they put her to sleep.

His wife had dreamed of her father in a coffin a few nights earlier, and it wasn't a good dream. She's been agitated for days.
And my friend's mother is also upset. They're having dinner together and she tells of another dream. She dreamed of her husband; but her husband has been gone for many years, and usually when she dreams of him ... someone ... She thinks her time has come, the time to join him.

It's not always easy to distinguish between dreams and symbols.

My friend starts praying for his father-in-law. Then he also prays for his mother. While praying, he feels that oppression, that strong oppression, the one he has been feeling for some time. The sensations are very clear and the sensations speak of something very bad. He has always entrusted himself to God's hands, to his will. If anything has to happen to my mother ...

I'm ready !

The next morning she was cold and he knew she was dead even before he touched her.

He screams!

No ! He's not ready for this.

He screams and runs ... They take the car ... Hospital.

Cerebral Death.

They call it white death. Death in the cradle.

Sleep apnea.

Why?
We are working for YOU.
Why us?

His faith is limitless. Faith forces you to believe before
understanding. Although it may seem absurd, we pray before the
funeral. Pray for the resurrection! The whole church, the flock,
comes together. If it happened once, it can happen again! They
pray for hours.

But ... The funeral is coming. He decides to speak at his
daughter's funeral. To preach at his daughter's funeral.
His legs are shaking. Lord, life for life ... a man is converted... but

He starts living in constant pain. He too wakes up at night with
tachycardia, and cries, cries a lot. Pain is always present.
And he understands that passage where it speaks of swords that
pierce the soul.

But he doesn't understand why, why those swords are theirs.

And the man of God is also a man and that's it.
You could have taken someone else.
He argues...
And he quarrels as Job did,

that he had done nothing wrong.

His strength is not enough.
His questions are unanswered.
His will is not enough to overcome that moment.
But faith does not collapse!
Keep believing even if you don't understand.
Keep asking questions, and getting no answers.
Just like Job:

"My spirit is broken, my days are cut short, the grave awaits me."

But the trials are never greater than those that can be endured for those who trust in him, and the way out arrives ...

Or escape ...

Keep helping others. Continue to preach, pray, support, marry and baptize.

Meanwhile, when my girlfriend leaves me, I can't even go to work, eat, breathe, he continues to serve. Keeps doing what he's called for.

The cyclone passes over him. It has been a disaster for more than a year. But he finally gets in the eye. And in the eye of the storm there is peace.

A passage from Isaiah arrives as a guarantee.
There will no longer be a child who lives only a few days; with the guarantees arrive two daughters. He smiles. They're really beautiful. But his eyes tremble when he talks about Sara.

There is little preparation. They're almost Jazz sermons.
Improvization. Inspiration of the moment. There was talk of

mourning. He had to lighten the burden of someone, someone of his flock. To do it... His eyes were trembling.

I have friends who ask me questions. I have friends to whom I answer, others to whom I don't. I've never tried to persuade anyone, but don't try to convince me with Darwin.
I'm not the son of pastors, but I'm the son of research, travel, mistakes, experiments. I'm the son of trials with religions, the son of reading and curiosity, the son of touching where you must not touch, and I was also the son of ... er ... the son of many doubts. But when I was chosen, the doubts vanished, forever, and if he tells me to demolish everything after he has had me build everything, I'll demolish everything ... And the pieces are mine. And if I see a bear enter my crystal shop, look at an ornament, touch it and break it, I don't care. The shards, the shop window, and even the clerk are where they need to be at that moment.

And even if you shake your head, laugh, and think that a monkey has become a man and a bear that has slept all night cannot be sleepy ...

Go ahead. Keep thinking about your crystals ...

Munnè is already thinking of mine ...

... and you are garbage too!

- Track 14 –

How many times ?

"We'll let you know ..."

... But no!

Grey. Not black or white. Grey.

My personal field statistics rattle off these numbers: out of a hundred interviews, meetings, auditions, casting, auditions, if it all ends with "We'll let you know", in 99% of cases, "We won't let you know". If you are the golden 0.1% of cases, "We will let you know" because you are the ones who need to know! In the other 0.9% "We'll let you know", with grace and education, that you are not the ones who need to know!

The courage of black represents the latter 0.9%.

The courage to look a person in the eye, shake his hand, but tell him no ... "You're not the person we're looking for" The courage to look a person in the eye and say: "I'm not in love with you! " The courage to look a person in the eye. Hold your gaze while you're hurting her.

We all have to evaluate someone sooner or later. The one who came with her punk boyfriend, and would like our son's apartment to rent, that in the meantime has changed to Casablanca "style". The one who will be the best candidate among all the unlikely who have presented themselves for our Alpine troop choir.

The one who could become the boom operator on a film set, and unfortunately only he's showed up and he's ugly too. The girl I've been dating for two months. She's good, she's beautiful, she comes from a good family and would never betray me.
But why isn't it my first thought in the morning and my last in the evening?

We have to take care of these things, not just those grim faces in "Personnel Selection"or "Human Resources".

There aren't many roads to choose from. Strong handshake or "can we talk later"? Look's at you directly or mirrored glasses? Addresses the problem or let's the other face it alone?

Hides behind unlikely "periods of reflection" or be firm, decisive, even when whoever we are facing does not deserve defeat, or victory?

"We'll let you know ..."

If you've already chosen,
you're gutless imbeciles!

We'll let you know!

Carnival Rides. As a child I loved rides, they made me feel great. Especially the bumper cars. You approached this big rectangle with loud music. Silver platforms around the perimeter. A couple of benches here and there. Then them: the colored, rubber bumpers; with the flag.

You sit in a seat, and you forget the color you have chosen. You're only interested in grabbing your first steering wheel. A plastic token slot and a nice pedal to ram yourself against others. Without any direction. Front, back, side, diagonally. Until everything stops. As long as you have tokens. Tokens to feel great.

The first time everything stopped, even though I was already grown, was against a light pole. It was where it was supposed to be ... But not me! I was in a dream world.

Eighteen years old. I thought I knew myself well. I thought I knew the world well. But I still didn't know that I was suffering from sleepiness while driving at night. Family members, friends, and even the light pole, all but one, always thought I was drunk.

End up with the pedal pressed against a light pole in the middle of a town, with no sign of having braked. What other explanation for an eighteen year old boy. But I remember well. I remember the street was deserted, and it was dark. It was the middle of the night and there was no one to play bumper cars with.

At one point I heard in the distance ... Glass. As if someone were throwing bottles two hundred meters away. It was in the distance. A very strange feeling, but clear. I remember it very well.

Then I'm awakened by "except one". He can touch me with his
hand. But, how does he do it, the door is closed ... and ... why's
the car radio dangling? "Hey guy ... Are you okay? ... Hey, like ... If
you have any weed, hide it because you fucked up here!" Weed?
But I don't smoke. What's he saying ? I get out of the car.
I understand that I have ended up against something. I stagger to
a phone booth. I call my parents. A tow truck arrives. Takes the
car away, and I just want to sleep. And I go to sleep as soon as I
get home.

The next day I let them take me to where they took the car ...
And fall to my knees!

The right front wheel was so close to the left that even the laws of
physics couldn't explain it. In the middle there was glass
everywhere. All completely smashed, like an empty tuna can,
flattened. In the middle, the driver's seat. Intact! I didn't have a
scratch!

I risked my life three times in a car.

The second with a car that was designed to never overturn. A '76
Citroen Dyane, sister of the more famous 2CV. Designed for
French peasants, who needed to be able to move between
potholes without breaking eggs. Engineers have shown that it's
easier to overturn a go-kart than a Citroen 2CV. Only two have
succeeded: one who took it as a personal challenge so he could
appear in online videos. He tried dozens of times and in the end
he only succeeded by driving it at the maximum possible speed,
in reverse, and then violently jerking the steering wheel. Easy
right?

And then me!

This time it was daylight, broad daylight, like two in the afternoon. On a Saturday afternoon. I was heading towards the town, a couple miles and a few hairpin bends further on. Cassette radio. What a cool tune. I look at the title a second. Just a second. I turn back to the windshield, and my car is at forty-five degrees.

Fucked.

You know those movies where the car hangs on a cliff. The car swings, but the protagonists are almost always saved. Here, I was the protagonist, but slowly ... Very slowly ... I understood that I could not have saved myself. Nothing to laugh about. Especially when the car overturned, and I was inside watching everything. It rolled, and did a couple of full flips before coming to a stop against a tree. And I screamed. I was screaming !!! And when the car stopped, and I was still upside down, I kept screaming. I was in shock, Total panic mode.

Inside the car there were branches, and the engine was still running. No one should ever have such an experience. No one should ever get distracted while driving. But I did, and I was screaming.

Somehow I get out of the car. I watch it. The wheels are still turning. There's a strange smell, a smell that shouldn't be in a forest. I climb up the slope. Someone sees me ... AND...

About two hours later two guys are drinking a beer at the bar. The small one on the corner of the intersection. They used to play football together.

They called themselves the 'brasileiru' clan. Now everyone has their own life for good or bad. Girlfriends, interests, different friends. But the blood link with the clan is forever. We grew up together, and you don't choose brothers. A tow truck goes by with a car on it ... and they run.

Ring the bell. They go up the stairs. They remain at the door. They see me safe and sound and ... Cile starts laughing; also Sergio. I don't have any fucking desire to laugh ... And they go back to the bar. First you run. And then you just laugh.

I've done a lot of stupid shit. Each of the clan has done a lot of stupid shit.

And the man in front of me has done a lot of stupid shit too. A man who waited to see if he was strong enough. Strong enough to walk alone, this time without fail.

Yes, because his biggest mistake was to do it alone. He thought he was the cleverest person in the world. He could have as much as he wanted, and when he wanted it. And being smart, he wouldn't get caught. And he never got caught!

He bought it out of town. Nobody knew who it was. He knew how not to be bugged on the phone, how not to go back by car, he explained things like a spy story. Everything to...

to calmly prepare before going to work. Early in the morning. Wake up half an hour earlier. The tinfoil. How he loves to smooth this tinfoil. It's very relaxing.

Then he heats it a bit to remove that crap smoke that only foil makes when it burns. Curves it like a capital U. Prepares a bus ticket, rolls it up, and makes the straw. Opens the cellophane. He takes that brown stone and puts it in the U. Quick heat to allow the little stone to melt a bit, a hair only, just to stick to the foil.

And then it begins ... It melts as if it were wax. A creme caramel wax to smoke with a bus ticket. He goes to work feeling invincible. After noon, before eating, another ticket for invincibility.

A few years of invincibility pass. He's young. He has many friends, but he doesn't talk about some things. He would risk getting caught ... And he, let's remember, never gets caught.

But the body begins to fail. There are times when the radiators flutter. Things vibrate. Maybe he doesn't feel so invincible anymore. He's realized for some time that he no longer smokes the U to feel good, but to survive the day. He's convinced that he must find a way to reduce the dose of invincibility. He succeeds a little. A week. But the week after ... Inertia. Survival mode.

He's a man who waited to see if he was strong enough. And when he realized that story had to end he also realized that he wasn't strong enough ... Alone.

The parents have noticed for a while that there is something wrong. It comes out at strange times. Speaks little. Eats little.

But they never caught him. He decides to open up to them. Also, to his girlfriend. She didn't even know.

He shakes off the inertia. The cards are now on the table. It took a lot of courage for a man used to doing everything alone. But now that his are discovered, how does he move? Nobody knew.

The family doctor recommends that place. The radio ad sketch. The one where there's always a junkie who takes methadone. The serT. He thought he would never, ever go there. An awful place full of junkies. And if they see you entering there, you're branded by those outside. But enter... He passes by the entrance over and over again to make sure no one sees him. With a newspaper open in front and with sunglasses and a cap pulled down on his head.

He enters.

Once again he'll never get caught!

Four years !

The first few times he feels very dirty. Take the flight of stairs with yellow walls to go to the second floor. Not the first, the one intended to for those who simply want to stop smoking and drinking. He has to go to the 'absolute quitters.' Heroes without heroin.

Then he gets used to being "inside". Inside it's not as dirty as he thought. He gets used to the coffee machine. To the many people sitting like they're waiting for a doctor. He gets used to being asked "Who's the last one?" to respect the queue.

He gets used to not being judged. He gets used to not being judged by those in the same boat, or even by the very polite people he finds inside the clinic. Nurses, secretaries, and then psychiatrists. Those who managed to undress the confident, well-dressed guy in front of them. They manage to get him to remove the ghosts, and help him put them back in the closet.

The helpfulness of the staff reassured him. He begins to feel more and more like a normal person. Not invincible but not judged. It's nice to be perfectly normal. And as a normal person he's met a fourteen-year-old boy, and his mom. And a seventy-five-year-old grandmother who doesn't go to accompany her grandson. Each time he stops for ten minutes, and in those ten minutes, he meets at least twenty people.

Start meeting acquaintances.
Unsuspected people.
The cashier of the supermarket.
The neighbor.
They're all "inside"
If they cross "outside",
they greet you politely. In secret.

He's seen too many people relapse quickly. Safe, invincible people who reduced their methadone dose too fast. They disappeared for a month and a half, and then they came back.

"Who's the last one?"

Yeah, methadone.

To stop one drug they had to take another, only instead of smoking it or injecting it, they had to drink it.

He was never in a hurry. They had foreseen a year for him, gradually reducing the daily dose to the mythical zero.

He preferred to take it slow, very slow. In the meantime things happen. The world around him had not stopped. Opportunities arrive. He tests himself. Calmly. Like things that are done well.

He has no relapses.

Never one.

He stays in the middle of shit but never gets dirty. Never once.

After four years he wants to prove his strength and constancy.
He's a man who waited to see if he was strong enough.
After four years he realizes that he would never have won alone.
Not without the help of the family and a couple of lovers.

Not without dialogue. Not without taking responsibility for it.

When he understood all this:
he won !

... And they never caught him.

He has a intense look. The man in front of me did a lot of stupid
shit. A man who waited to see if he was strong enough. Strong
enough to walk alone, this time without fail.
————

I'm at the usual bar, at the usual corner of the intersection, with
two of the clan. We're having a cool summer beer on a normal
Saturday afternoon. We're just over twenty years old. We grew up
together. We understand each other with looks. There are a lot of
other people around us. People we don't know. People having
normal beer on a normal Saturday afternoon.

A police patrol passes by. They're doing their job. They patrol the
area. They notice our table. They notice one of us. They stop the
car. They come down. They're coming closer.

He wasn't doing anything. He was talking to me and another of
the clan. He hadn't been doing anything for years. But a few years
earlier they had caught him. He had a intense look. He had done a
lot of stupid shit. He had waited to see if he was strong enough.
Strong enough to walk alone. He was no longer wrong.

They make him stand up in front of everyone. In front of a lot of
people we don't know on a normal Saturday afternoon.
They smile and ask for his documents. They check them ... and
they leave ...

with our smiles.

They're doing their job. They patrol the area. But nobody at our table deserved to be noticed. No more than the unknown ones around us.
One of us didn't deserve that document check. In the midst of regular people who judged and condemned with their eyes.
And he had checks all the time, even if he was no longer wrong. They never checked us. Always only him. Who was strong enough to walk alone without fail.

After a while, my friend from the clan gets tired. He can no longer be looked at as the one who does stupid shit. He's done a lot, but now he's a man.

He decides not to be seen around much anymore.

I'm going to find him. We grew up together. He doesn't tell me anything. We understand each other with looks.

I go out and cry!

A week goes by. Ring the bell. They go up the stairs. They remain on the door. There are always two. This time Cile is missing ... and no one start's laughing.

I risked my life three times in a car.
Although I knew I suffered from sleepiness while driving at night, I was far from home and wanted to get there. I enter a tunnel. The yellow lights become lines that turn white and ... is... And I feel a slap. A very strong slap!

I wake up and straighten the car as it's about to crash at eighty miles an hour.

It was in the distance. A very strange but clear feeling. I remember it very well ...

Cile saved my life ...

- Track 1 –

Time !

It didn't take them ninety days, it took a lot less.

They have already chosen after about thirty days.

And between life or death, there have been many punches! Lots of suffering. I took all those blows myself ... ... and she did too.

Time !

I took a ride to the police. Out of there, more punches. I took a ride to the doctor ... and more blows. Lots of jabs.

Kids. It would be more accurate to say a boy and a girl.

He stops at the front gate of the house, gets out of the car and starts screaming. He doesn't enter but screams. Maybe he respects the father. Not the son.

He calls him, screams at him, provokes him. Meanwhile, blows. The son gets out and the father gets out too. Two men face off. Still fighting.

Time !

The boy he's looking for is twenty years old.

The little girl in the car, is his daughter, and is fifteen.

They have already decided after thirty days. They loved each other. They kept the son! They never thought of any other alternative.

From love to the police? Thirty days counting.

It's been difficult. It was all damn hard. They were young. They were awfully young. But they decided to get married.

From beatings to marriage? Thirty days.

The honeymoon a few miles from where I live now. Just three or four more. A tourist hotel on the right records their first steps.

Uphill !

Now they laugh, but only at those precious moments.

From love to beatings? Thirty days. From beatings to marriage? Thirty days. Therefore: from love to marriage? Sixty days!

The length prediction of all marriages between sheep?

Six months at best.
Actual duration of the marriage?
Forty-four years with no expiration date.

Kids. It would be more accurate to say a boy and a girl.
They're laughing. He remembers and she presses him.
Beatings. Lots of beatings.

I struggle.

I can hardly believe it!

But I know it's true.

I know it's all damn true.

A boy: Guido Perino ... My father
A little girl: Immacolata Nardiello ... My mother.

Between life or death, they chose life.

Between my life or my death ...

They chose my life.

Two black sheep.

I am a choice!

I was born a sheep!

Bleat and shit balls.

They're like all of you. Not better, not worse. A sheep !

One day I found myself alone.

Then something happened.

I felt eyes on me.

They pointed at me.

I stood still and one by one they calmly approached.

They were sheep like all the others. Not better, not worse. Sheep!

They looked at me a bit strange at first. Curious. Then one by one they started looking for clumps of grass around me.

Bleating and shitting balls ...

... black

- Thanks and Credits -

Every story is true. These are not fictional stories. I've met all the people I've written about. Some I knew before the writing of the book, others I met for the book. I tried not to make judgments when listening to what I was told. I'm not a journalist, maybe I'm not even a writer. I'm a person who has many doubts, who has made a lot of mistakes and will still make mistakes. Sometimes I don't understand if I'm wrong or not. This book is a "sometimes I don't understand". I pray to God every day to show me the way. The signs have not always been clear. Sometimes they have been, sometimes not. When they were and they were a No, I didn't hesitate for a single moment to tear up what I had written. I was incredibly lucid, neutral, impartial. Almost frightening. I've tried to write under these conditions. Without judgment. I simply put the sheets on the table to be read by you. I couldn't afford to cry. I didn't cry once ... Alone !

I want to thank all the people who opened up looking me in the eye, trusting me, and putting their life in my hands. By putting their life in *your* hands. Before everyone else, those people who cannot be named, due to legal problems or the fact that by naming them they would compromise the lives of other people around them. To you… Friends… Thank you! Your anonymity is the most precious thing I will guard!

I also thank all those people who then ... Then they didn't feel like telling all. Your stories will remain yours. The emotions you gave me will remain mine.

Then thank you, I'll absolutely shuffle in order:

God, as my Best Friend… Thanks for letting me know when to tear!
My father in the role as my father.
My mother in the role as as my mother,
and my mother in the role of my mother wants to thank all the staff of the Parma Hospital:
"YOU ARE FANTASTIC ! "

My sister as my sister, and my brother-in-law as my sister's boyfriend
Marika and Samuele in the shoes of the two sheep they have generated.
Enrico Montesin in the role of Trinca.
The Vittorio Giovannacci bookshop as the bookshop where I bought two or
three Asimov's books.
Vilma, Elisa Giovannacci and Federico Bertuzzi in the roles of the greatest
who are always the most humble.
Alessandro Lualdi in the role of Mr Neutral.
Sara Rubele as the jealous girlfriend of Mr Neutral, her alpha male.
My gastrocnemius muscle as my gastrocnemius muscle.
Vladimir Jancarik as the friend who made us chase the police car.
Enrico Gariazzo in the role of Hard Haid Moe
Turgay Ünsal and Özge Dülger as those who made me understand how
beautiful the Islamic world can be.
Diana as the bearer of Dave.
Dave as whoever married Diana.
Andrea Guasco in the role of the demiurge.
Guido Nardi in the shoes of the sneaky.
All the smiles of the inmates and prison guards of the Biella Prison.
Marilise Scorteccia in the shoes of the one who made me open the doors to
this world, realizing my great little dream.
Valeria Treccani in the role of Meryl Streep.
The woodworm man in the shoes of man.
The woodworm in the role of the woodworm.
My uncles, cousins, nephews, distant relatives, neighbors, southerners,
polentoni, foreigners, sideways, up and down, in the shoes of the most
uncoordinated family that could happen to me.
Andrea Figus and La Masca in the role of those who had the unconsciousness
to follow "Little Dreams"; I'm already calling my lawyer.
Alessio Ciapponi as my lawyer.
The Boney M as the Boney M with Rivers of Babylon Words.
Enrico Caputo as the guitarist who borrowed the first dusty piano for me.
Sophie as the virgin until she gets married.
The Capuchin friar in the role of the man who slaps one on the back.

Giuseppe Simonetti for leading me to the great shepherd and for contributing immensely.

"Hunger for Grass" with Gianfranco Bini and Giorgina Viquèry.

Erika Magnani for all the messages and phone calls and indications from shepherds, in the end we did it!

All the bikers and especially the colors of the Steel Roses MC group, you've always respected me as a biker without a bike, the signs were clear, I had to give up on being a biker.

The mother and the child of 15 per hour, I don't remember what they are called, but they're there in front of the whole queue.

Corrado Maggia in the role of the shepherd from the Jazz sermons.

Anna Maria Bosio as the Jazz pastor's wife.

Ted Martin Consoli because you always smile, and whoever always smiles should be thanked.

Ted's parents, Anna and Claude ... What ... What a load of stuff.

Munnè in the role of garbage ... And you are garbage too!

SIO in the role of the man who never gets caught.

111 shades of Black as The Duck Avenger

Fabio Aguzzoli in the role of the artist truck driver who does shiatsu while also doing photography and in the meantime he is a quiet one without too many worries in his head.

Don Mario Coppo in the role of that little man there.

Renato Garrione, in the role of the literature teacher of middle school who laughs with the priest, and in the role of the one who still reads my manuscripts today.

I am writing thanks to you Renato… Remember that!

Catia in the role of the professor's wife who smiles every time I pick up the phone, and who makes me smile every time she makes me sit at their table.

Frix and Chiara, Roberto and Sonia, Cinghios and Mirela, Paolo and Simo and your myriads of little children, in the roles of my friends coupled and happy, for all the times you shake your head talking to me.

Puzzle as my black cat.

Caramel as Ely's cat who is now mine as well.

Elisa, Giada, Elena and whoever happens to be Koolo, we're the best rock band.
Elena Quaglia in the role of Elena ...
As a professional educator she failed with me, but with others she is fantastic!
She is the most ohm woman of any Zen woman that exists ...!

In memory of Gianni Ursella, my neighbor who learned the computer by pouring me some white wine.
And...
In memory of the best football team of all time ...
 "The brasileiru clan":
Giancarlo Lovison, Sergio Contato, Luca and Stefano Grassetto, Fabio and Christian Beninati,
Vobevto Cagna Bvoglio, in goal I and ...
Marco "CILE" Cilento making a mess ...

And I thank you too ...

You who now have doubts ...

What if the black sheep is...   ..?

INDEX:

Marco Perino, born in Gattinara in 1974.
He has always lived in small villages in the province of Biella, "Base Camp" city where he loves to return after every adventure.

Musician, author, teacher, and writer.

By the same author:

"Little Dreams" (2013)

"... What if the black sheep is me?" (2017)

"Orange" (2020)

https://www.facebook.com/marcoperinobooks/